WHAT
ARIA
COOKING?

San Francisco Opera Cookbook

1974

$800—

7/24

Production By: David Charlsen
                 Planned Production/Douglas Mount And Others

Special Thanks to: Jacqueline Cozad, Mark Behrens,
                   Deborah Johansen

Composition: WB Associates/Mel Salman

Library of Congress Catalog Card Number: 74-10605

Standard Book Number: 0-9600758-1-X

Printed in the United States of America

First Printing

Casey, Donna, comp.
   What aria cooking?

     1. Cookery.   I. San Francisco Opera Guild Auxiliary.   II. Title.
TX715.C425   641.5   74-10605
ISBN 0-9600758-1-X

FOREWORD

This book is a special collection of favorite recipes by opera personalities who have contributed to the growth of the San Francisco Opera Company and, indeed, the city itself as an international cultural center. There are many facets of San Francisco Opera—aside from the regular fall season. There are the Western Opera Theater, Spring Opera and the Merola Opera programs.

We have included recipes from singers in each company, as well as some from production and administrative personalities.

The enthusiasm of the contributors was boundless—and we thank them for their interest and response.

We hope the users of the book will enjoy the recipes and realize they are contributing to the enrichment of opera in the San Francisco community.

CURTAIN CALL: The last section of the book is a catchall of menus and favorite restaurants the contributors frequent during the season.

Edited by: Donna M. Casey
for: The San Francisco Opera Guild Auxiliary
Illustrations by: Fifi Holbrook
Front cover photo: San Francisco Visitors Bureau
Back photo: Lyman H. Casey

EDITOR'S NOTE

This book is the result of the enthusiasm and support of many people and I should like to thank each of them—but it would be impossible, in this limited space to list them all.

Blanche Koenig, President of the San Francisco Opera Guild and the Board of Directors encouraged us in our endeavor and gave us the support needed to complete the book.

The San Francisco Opera Guild Auxiliary should be commended for their patience in listening to me, for their enthusiasm in writing and talking to the artist-contributors, for their time in testing recipes in their own kitchens and for their determination to sell the book.

Special thanks are due to Kurt Herbert Adler, General Director of the San Francisco Opera, and his wife Nancy; Kori Lockhart and the Publicity Department of the San Francisco Opera; Mary Packard, Secretary to the San Francisco Opera Guild; Fawcett Publications for editorial assistance; William Duncan Allen, Colin Harvey, Scott Martin, Alexandra Remmel—all of whom were constantly available with assurance, help and who had answers to all sorts of questions. The lovely illustrations by my even lovelier friend, Fifi Holbrook, deserve tremendous praise!

Lastly, I should like to thank my husband and children for allowing me to ignore them while the book was in the making.

Extensive musical education from elementary school to the college level sounds impossible, but the San Francisco Opera Guild is trying hard to accomplish this, at least in the field of opera education, with its Opera for Students Program.

Since its inception in 1939 the program has enabled over 325,000 students to hear opera. Five matinees are presented to the students during the fall season after an in-school preparatory lesson taught by Guild volunteers. The Guild is responsible for funding the operas as well as contributing to the San Francisco Opera Association. To date, over $450,000 has gone to that organization from Guild fund raising efforts.

The San Francisco Opera Guild Auxiliary was started in 1969 as an adjunct to the Guild Board. The original eleven women have expanded to forty active volunteers involved in every facet of the Board's work. This book was conceived and produced by the Auxiliary as its own fund raising effort. Proceeds of this book will go to a special Opera program for students. The Guild plans to expand the present program to allow handicapped and deprived children to attend the student matinees.

Officers

Chairman: Mrs. David S. Hanna
Vice Chairman: Mrs. Lyman H. Casey
Recording Secretary: Mrs. Thomas Fawcett
Corresponding Secretary: Mrs. Peter Holbrook

Mrs. R. Lawrence Bacon
Miss Joan Baron
Mrs. Ralph Bastian
Mrs. Per Borgen
Mrs. Theodore Burgess
Mrs. Robert Todd Cary
Mrs. Lyman H. Casey
Mrs. A. Lawrence Chickering
Mrs. H. A. Chickering
Miss Joan H. Cochran
Mrs. David Duxbury
Mrs. Thomas C. Escher
Mrs. Thomas Fawcett
Miss Meade Funsten
Mrs. Dirk H. W. Garshagen
Mrs. Thomas G. Griffith
Mrs. David S. Hanna
Mrs. Reeve Hennion
Mrs. Peter M. Holbrook
Mrs. James E. Hotle
Mrs. Howard A. Huenergardt
Mrs. William J. Hume
Mrs. W. James Kempenich
Mrs. William Randolph Leathers, II
Mrs. W. Patrick McDowell
Miss Marian Miller

ARTIST'S INDEX

Adler, Kurt Herbert
Albanese, Licia

Alexander, John
Allen, Betty
Atherton, James
Alvary, Lorenzo
Arroyo, Martina
Berberian, Ara

Blegen, Judith
Bogard, Carol
Bryn-Jones, Delme

Bumbry, Grace

Burgess, Gary
Bybee, Ariel
Capobianco, Tito
Cassily, Richard
Cervena, Sona
Clark, Richard
Cossa, Dominic
Curzi, Cesare
Dalis, Irene

Dooley, William
Drake, Archie

Emoed-Wallace, Julia
Eybel, Querita (Houdlette)
Flagello, Ezio
Gobbi, Tito
Grant, Clifford
Harness, William
Hecht, Joshua
Hooper, James
Hoskinson, Orva

Vanilleknipferl
Linguine alla Licia Albanese
Risotto Milanese
Black Bottom Pie
Crabmeat Casserole
Litvac
Filet of Sole
Fresh Crab Dish
Bulghour Pilaf
Tutmaj (Yogurt Soup)
Persian Rice
Pollo a lo Agridulce
Roast Snipe
Welsh Cheese Pudding
Shrimp Creole in
    Spinach and Rice Ring
Sour Cream Potato Soup
Sour Cream Custard Pie
Spaghetti alla Capobianco
Yogurt Soup
Czech Fruit Dumpling
Chicken Surprise
Casalinga
Pepper Steak
Caponatina
Greek Cookies
Keftethakia
Mexican Salad
Oxtail in Wine
Curtain Call
Szegedi Gulyas
Dream Balls
Egg Noodles alla Bolognese
Pasta alla Tito Gobbi
Pavlova Cake
Smothered Steak Roll-ups
Spaghetti alla Matriciana
Divine Crabmeat Casserole
Oatmeal Cake
Broil-on-Icing

Langdon, Michael	*Curtain Call*
Lawrence, Douglas	*Rock Cornish Hens*
Lear, Evelyn	*Beefsteak Woronoff*
	Granita di Caffe
London, George	*Southern Pecan Pie*
Ludgin, Chester	*Veal Cutlets in Port*
Malas, Spiro	*Crab Cake Puffs*
	Curtain Call
	Dolmades with Lemon Sauce
	Greek Salad
	Keftethakia
	Moussaka
	Sukiyaki on the Road
Malucelli, Ken	*Bachelor's Cake*
	Die Miestersalad
	Florian Fruit Salad Dressing
	Frulato
	Morning Fruit Bread
Manton, Raymond	*Curtain Call*
Matsumoto, Shigemi	*Tempura*
McCracken, James	*Tonno-Mariner's Style*
McGuckin, Henry	*Almond Bavarois with Choco-* *late Sauce*
	Eggplant Pizzas
	Fish Sauce Lasagna
Meier, Johanna	*Linsensuppe (Lentil Soup)*
Milanov, Zinka	*Bourex (Cheese Pastry* *Fingers)*
	String Beans Yugoslave
Moffo, Anna	*Cannelloni*
Mosley, Robert	*Saltimbocca a la Mosli*
Mundt, Richard	*Blitzen Torte*
	Porkloin and Red Cabbage
Patenande, Joan	*Beef Bourguignon*
Pavarotti, Luciano	*Curtain Call*
	Fresh Fruit
	Maltaliati con Fagioli
	Pavarotti Cocktail
Peerce, Jan	*Chicken in the Pot*
	Potato Kugel
	Russian and Oriental *Eggplant*
Peress, Maurice	*Stuffed Cabbage*
Petersen, Donna	*Cherry Cheesecake Pie*
	Italian Delight

Price, Leontyne	Crabmeat Imperial Casserole
	Curtain Call
Reardon, John	Beet and Endive Salad
	Cold Tomato Soup
Riegal, Kenneth	Amish Cabbage with Sour Cream and Bacon
	Hot Endive Salad
	Pennsylvania Dutch Corn Chowder
	Snitz and Knepp
Roberts, Rebecca	Standing Room Chicken
Roman, Stella	Romanian Walnut Croissants
Saroya, Bianca	Bermuda Drink
	Chicken Bombay
	Epicurian Cocktail
Sayao, Bidu	Mousse de Chocolat
Schwabacher, James	Creme de Tomate Marie-Louise
Silja, Anja	Curtain Call
Sills, Beverly	Hollandaise Sauce
Singher, Martial	Chicken and Pear Mousse
Steber, Eleanor	Chicken and Lobster Cantonese
Stewart, Thomas	Dill and Pepper Cured Salmon
	Dill and Mustard Sauce
	Granita di Caffe
Sze, Yi Kwei	Shrimp a la Sze
Thebom, Blanche	Poulet a la Couchet Blanche
Thomas, Jess	Beef Tea
Tucker, Richard	Carrot, Sweet Potato and Prune Tzimmes
Van Staade, Frederica	Cold Pea Soup
von Buchau, Stephanie	Linguine with White Clam Sauce
Yarnell, Bruce	Beef Bourguignon
	Caesar Salad
	Cafe Brûlot
Zylis-Gara, Teresa	Lamb-filled Ravioli

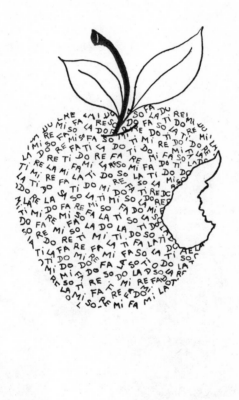

11

Overture

BERMUDA DRINK

BIANCA SAROYA

Ginger beer (in crocks) plus rum and lime to taste.

EPICURIAN COCKTAIL

BIANCA SAROYA

Equal amounts of Sloe gin and Bourbon with a small amount of sugar and lemon.

LITVAK

JAMES ATHERTON

1 *part Sabra*
2 *parts Vodka*

Shake with ice. Strain.

PAVAROTTI COCKTAIL

LUCIANO PAVAROTTI

mineral water
dry Lambrusco

BEEF TEA

JESS THOMAS

1 *pound top sirloin steak*
water
salt

Trim the meat of all fat and, using a very sharp knife, shave the meat into slivers. Pack the meat slivers into a Mason jar, cover, and place the jar into a heavy saucepan filled with water. Do not add any water to the meat itself. The water in the saucepan should reach the level of the meat in the jar. Allow the water to simmer on very low heat for 3 to 4 hours, being careful never to let the water boil. Decant the tea and salt to taste. It can be drunk warm or cold.

Yields one cup.

Just before a performance, Thomas drinks a beef tea for extra energy. Actually, the tea is an infusion of pure beef extract, and Thomas says that it supplies exactly the same kind of lift that prizefighters get from chewing raw or partially cooked meat. He learned the preparation form his grandmother. It is nourishment without bulk and a strength builder. Thomas' beef tea is a welcome suggestion when heavy work beckons. And, of course, if you want to impress guests with a truly imaginative soup, this is the answer.

BOUREK
(CHEESE PASTRY FINGERS)

ZINKA MILANOV

1 *tablespoon butter*
1 *tablespoon flour*
¼ *teaspoon salt*
few grains pepper
¼ *cup milk*
¼ *pound Gruyere-type cheese*
½ *recipe for plain pastry*

Melt butter, add flour, salt and pepper; blend. Add milk. Stir over low heat until thickened. Cut cheese in small pieces; add to mixture. Stir until cheese melts. Chill. Shape in small rolls about 4 inches long and ¼ inch in diameter. Roll pastry very thin and cut in oblongs about 4¼ inches long and ¾ inches wide. Wrap each cheese roll in a pastry oblong. Pinch edges together. Fry in shallow fat heated to 370° F. for 3 to 4 minutes, or until golden brown. Serve hot.

Approximate yield: 24 cheese pastry fingers.

SHRIMP A LA SZE

YI KWEI SZE

Jumbo Shrimp, shelled and deveined. Slit down the back and lay flat. Sprinkle with garlic salt and a little sherry. Make a thin batter of the following:

1 *egg*
flour
bacon
dash of salt to taste
dash of monosodium glutamate

Dip shrimp into batter, wrap each shrimp in bacon leaving only the ends showing. Lay on broiler rack and broil quickly, until bacon is brown, turning once. Garnish and serve immediately as a fish entree. May also be used as an hors d'oeuvre cut into bite-size pieces.

CAPONATINA
(SICILIAN EGGPLANT RELISH)

IRENE DALIS

1 *large eggplant*
1 *cup diced celery*
  salt
  olive oil for frying
1 *large onion, sliced thin*
½ *cup Spanish olives, pitted and sliced*
2 *tablespoons capers*
2 *level tablespoons sugar*
½ *cup wine vinegar*
1 *cup tomato puree*

Dice the eggplant, leaving skin on. Sprinkle with salt and place in a colander. Place a very heavy plate or skillet over the colander to press the eggplant down. Let it stand this way for about an hour so the water will drain from it. Pat the pieces dry with absorbent paper. Simmer the celery in unsalted water to cover for ten minutes. Reserve the celery and water. Slowly brown the eggplant in the olive oil in a large, deep skillet. Put the eggplant aside and lightly brown the onion in the same skillet. Add the olives, capers, sugar, the cooked celery with its liquid, and the eggplant. Simmer for 15 minutes, stirring occasionally. Let mixture cool. Caponatina can be stored in the refrigerator for at least a week. With antipasto, it is served on small crisp crackers. It is also excellent as a cocktail spread.

Serves eight.

CASALINGA

DOMINIC COSSA

½ *pound chicken livers*
1 *large onion*
4 *tablespoons oil*
4 *tablespoons chili sauce*
2 *tablespoons capers*
⅛ *teaspoon Accent*
⅛ *teaspoon garlic salt*
  salt and pepper to taste

Saute onion in 2 tablespoons oil until golden. Remove from pan. Wash livers; dry well, and add to pan with another 1 tablespoon oil. Sprinkle Accent and saute, ten minutes, then cool slightly. Using fine grinder or food chopper, grind livers, onions, and capers together. Stir in chili sauce, salt and pepper to taste, and garlic salt. Allow to stand overnight. To serve, heat with 1 tablespoon oil over low heat, stirring. Serve hot with small rounds of sliced french bread.

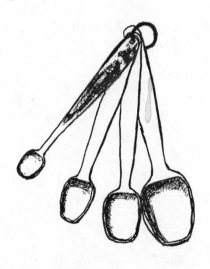

KEFTETHAKIA
(GREEK MEATBALLS)

SPIRO MALAS

1½ pounds ground meat (round or chuck)
  1 cupful breadcrumbs browned lightly in dry
    frying pan
  1 egg
  5 black olives, pitted and finely chopped
  1 big onion finely chopped
3-4 sprigs chopped parsley, preferably the
    Italian kind with big flat leaves
5-6 leaves fresh basil, or 1 tablespoon dried
    half a nutmeg, ground
  1 tablespoon salt
    fresh ground pepper to taste
    olive oil and butter for cooking

Soak the browned breadcrumbs in water or white wine and
squeeze out most of the fluid. Mix all the ingredients using your
hands. Let rest a little before you make about 50 small meatballs.
Roll them in fine breadcrumbs and a tablespoon or two of flour
mixed in before you saute them in the olive oil and butter you
have already melted in a heavy iron frying pan.

EGGPLANT PIZZAS

HENRY MC GUCKIN

1 *medium or large eggplant*
1 or 2 *cans Marinara Sauce*
seasoned bread crumbs
8 to 12 *ounces mozarella cheese*
2 *large baking dishes*
grated parmesan cheese
flour
2-3 *eggs*
salad or olive oil

Slice eggplant. Salt each slice. Let stand for 20 minutes. Drain liquid and dry each slice. Dip each slice into flour, beaten eggs, bread crumbs in that order. Fry in oil over moderate heat until golden. Put a thin layer of marinara sauce into each greased baking dish. Cover each eggplant slice with a slice of mozarella cheese. Cover with remaining marinara sauce and sprinkle with parmesan cheese. Bake, uncovered, for 20 to 30 minutes.

Serves four to six.

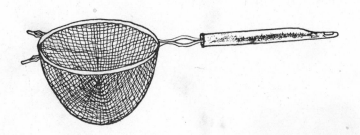

CRAB CAKE PUFFS

SPIRO MALAS

1 *pound crab meat*
½ *cup soft bread crumbs*
3 *teaspoons chopped parsley*
1 *egg*
1 *teaspoon dry mustard*
1 *teaspoon Worcestershire sauce*
  mayonnaise

Mix crab meat with soft bread crumbs and chopped parsley. Add egg and dry mustard and Worcestershire sauce and enough mayonnaise to moisten.

Shape the crab mixture about the size of golf balls. Combine the following ingredients for a thick batter:

2 *cups flour*
1 *egg*
1 *teaspoon salt*
1 *teaspoon seafood seasoning*
½ *teaspoon white pepper*
  pinch of baking soda
  water

Dip each crab cake in the batter and deep fry in fat heated to 350° until browned and puffed.

KEFTETHAKIS
(MEATBALLS)

IRENE DALIS

1 *pound ground round steak*
6 *small slices whole wheat bread, toasted*
1 *egg, slightly beaten*
1 *teaspoon olive oil*
1 *small onion, chopped fine*
1 *teaspoon lemon juice*
1 *tablespoon chopped parsley*
1 *tablespoon chopped basil*
¼ *teaspoon nutmeg*
   salt and pepper to taste
   oil and butter for sauteing

Soak the toast in water and squeeze dry. Mix all ingredients thoroughly, kneading the mixture with the hands for 3 to 4 minutes. Let the mixture stand for ½ hour. Form into bite-sized balls and roll lightly in fine bread crumbs. Saute the balls in equal amounts of oil and butter until browned. Yields approximately 3 dozen.

Serves eight.

Soups

COLD TOMATO SOUP

JOHN REARDON

Equal parts of:
>*canned cream of tomato soup*
>*buttermilk*

Add to taste:
>*curry powder*
>*lemon slices*

Mix (in a blender, if possible) equal parts of canned cream of tomato soup and buttermilk. Add curry powder to taste (as "hot" as you can stand). Store the soup in the refrigerator overnight. Serve cold, with a slice of lemon on top.

Just a suggestion: For a quick Sunday brunch, make a platter of toasted cheese sandwiches to go with the soup. It's great!

COLD PEA SOUP

FREDERICA VAN STAADE

1 *can (10^1/$_3$ oz.) green pea soup*
^{1}/$_3$ *cup champagne*
fresh mint
½ *pint whipping cream*
½ *cup milk or cream*
salt and pepper
fresh tarragon

Steep half a tablespoon of fresh chopped mint and tarragon in 3 tablespoons of warm water for ½ hour. Strain the contents, and to the liquid, add 1 can of pea soup. Stir over heat and add ½ cup of milk or cream.

Pour contents into a pitcher and refrigerate until icy cold. Before serving add chilled champagne, pour into soup cups and put a tablespoon of whipped cream in the center of each cup as well as some chopped mint as garnish.

YOGURT SOUP

RICHARD CASSILLY

2½ quarts beef stock
½ cup Greek Pasta (hard wheat grits)
10-15 small quarter-sized meatballs
4 cups yogurt
½ cup melted butter
¼ cup lemon juice
1½ tablespoon dried mint leaves
garlic, salt, and pepper

Prepare ahead of time small meat balls. Use lean ground beef and season with garlic, dried mint, salt and pepper.

Into the boiling stock pour the wheat shaped pasta, meatballs and salt and pepper. When these are done, remove pan from fire and allow to cool slightly. Add yogurt. Keep hot but DO NOT BOIL. Combine melted butter, lemon juice, and mint leaves. Serve soup immediately and float lemon-butter-mint sauce on each individual portion.

PENNSYLVANIA-DUTCH CORN CHOWDER

KENNETH RIEGEL

4 *slices bacon*
1 *tablespoon minced celery*
1 *tablespoon minced green pepper*
1 *tablespoon onion*
2 *potatoes*
3 *tomatoes*
2 *cups of cooked corn kernels, fresh from the cob*
2 *pints of milk or 1 pint each of milk and light cream*
1 *cup water*
salt and pepper

Chop bacon and place in pan to brown. Add minced celery, pepper and onion, fry together until bacon is brown. Add corn and saute together for 3 minutes. Add the chopped vegetables and 1 cup water. Cover and cook slowly for 30 minutes. Add rich milk and heat to boiling again. Add chopped parsley (optional.)
   Serves four.

SOUR CREAM POTATO SOUP

GARY BURGESS

6 *potatoes, peeled and cut*
4 *cups of water*
2 *teaspoons of salt*
2½ *tablespoons whole allspice*
5 *whole cloves*

Place spices in tea pod or tie in cheese cloth and cook with potatoes, water and salt, until potatoes are done. Allow spices to stay in soup mixture 1½ hours, before removing.

Add 16 ounces of sour cream, and 2 teaspoons of lemon juice. Mash potatoes if you want soup smoother. Heat to just below boiling point. Serve. To make richer or "stretch" add canned milk and lemon juice or more sour cream. Flavor improves if soup is not served immediately.

CREME DE TOMATE MARIE-LOUISE

JAMES SCHWABACHER

1 *tablespoon butter*
1 *tablespoon flour*
1 *can (14 oz.) tomato juice*
½ *cup milk*
1 *teaspoon sugar*
  a pinch of baking soda
  pepper
  salt
  cinnamon
  lemon peel twist
  stalk of celery with tops
  parsley root or chopped parsley

Melt one healthy tablespoon of butter and add one tablespoon flour. Stir well over medium flame and do not let the butter brown. Then add the can of tomato juice. Season to taste with the pepper, salt, cinnamon, lemon peel twist, stalk of celery, and parsley. Then add one teaspoon of sugar and stir. Bring to a boil and simmer until well flavored. Skim to remove vegetables and lemon peel. Place in a double boiler until ready to serve. When ready to serve, add a pinch of baking soda and the half a cup of milk. Stir gently over low flame.

Serves three.

YOGURT SOUP
(TUTMAJ)

ARA BERBERIAN

1 *egg beaten*
3 *cups yogurt*
2 *cups water*
1 *small onion, finely diced*
1 *teaspoon salt*
6 *tablespoons butter*
2 *tablespoons crushed dry mint*
$1/3$ *cup small square egg noodles*

Mix egg, yogurt and salt in a 2 quart saucepan. Beat three minutes. Cook on a fast fire, stirring until boiling. Add noodles, lower fire, and cook until tender. Saute the onions in the butter in a frying pan until light brown then add the mint. Pour into the soup, cook together for five minutes. In case the soup becomes too thick for the next day's serving, add some boiling water.

Serves eight.

LINSENSUPPE
(LENTIL SOUP)

JOHANNA MEIER

2 *cups dried lentils*
  handful chopped fresh parsley
1 *chopped onion*
3 *large stalks of celery*
  salt to taste
  ham knuckle or ham bone
3 *bay leaves*
2 *sliced carrots*
1 *sprinkling of dill*
  slices of lemon

Wash and drain lentils. Soak them in large covered pan with meaty ham bone, replenishing water as it is soaked up (for several hours or overnight). Then begin to simmer over low flame adding the handful of chopped parsley and three quarts water, the three bayleaves, and the sprinkling of dill. As the mixture thickens, add salt to taste—depending on how much of the salty ham flavor is present. As beans soften, press them frequently against the side of the pot to mash them and pry loose ham chunks from the bone. Add the sliced carrots and the chopped onion. One hour before serving add the chopped celery stalks including the leaves. Cook all day over very low flame, stirring and mashing frequently. Remove ham bone and serve hot with slices of lemon floating on top.

CARROT-SWEET POTATO-PRUNE TZIMMES

RICHARD TUCKER

1 *pound soup meat*
7 *large carrots*
2 *large sweet potatoes*
8 *prunes*
1 *tablespoon finely cut onion*
1 *pinch of ginger*
½ *tablespoon cornstarch*
½ *cup brown sugar*
½ *cup honey*
1 *tablespoon salt*

Cover meat in boiling water. Add onion and salt, cook forty-five minutes. Add carrots cut in rounds about ¾ inches, cut potatoes in large chunks, add sugar, ginger, prunes, honey. Again add ½ glass of water and cook till tender. Then mix cornstarch with water until smooth. Also, add some of the carrot water. Mix in and cook until really soft another fifteen minutes.

Serves six to eight.

Vegetables & Salads

DIE MEISTERSALAD

KEN MALUCELLI

Use two heads each of lettuce in salad. In a very large bowl combine torn tops of red lettuce, torn fresh spinach and parsley, torn hearts of romaine and butter lettuce. Add ¼ cup each crumbled blue cheese, crumbled cheddar cheese, six pieces well-cooked bacon, crumbled, 4 chopped green onions, 1 stalk diced celery, ½ can drained, chopped anchovies, six to eight stemmed, slit and drained Pepperoncine, ½ sliced cucumber, and the following herbs:

> 1 *teaspoon Italian salad herbs*
> ½-1 *teaspoon dill weed*
> ½ *teaspoon tarragon*
> *several dashes of Beau Monde seasoning*
> *garlic salt*
> *onion salt*

Toss to blend all ingredients. In a large wooden bowl, lined with lettuce leaves, pour in the above mixture. On top arrange halved cherry tomatoes, avocado slices, hard-boiled egg quarters and pimiento and green pepper slices. Bring to table, and with a flourish splash on vinegar, olive oil, ground fresh pepper and a dash of salt.

STAND BACK AND WATCH THE RAVES

YUGOSLAVIAN STRING BEANS

ZINKA MILANOV

1½ *pounds string beans*
¼ *pound butter or chicken fat*
1 *big clove garlic, chopped*
4 *ounces sour cream*
2 *tablespoons breadcrumbs*
½ *bunch parsley, chopped*

Cook one and one-half pounds of young string beans in the usual way in fast-boiling, salted water, removing and draining the moment they become tender. Melt a quarter pound of butter or chicken fat in a pan over the fire, and when it not only melts but becomes golden, add 2 tablespoons of bread crumbs and let them brown, stirring so the browning is even. Meanwhile, you have finely chopped half a bunch of parsley leaves, not stems, and added to it a big clove of garlic, cut up then pounded and mashed. Pepper the mixture and mix well with the fried bread crumbs, then remove pan from fire. Add this bread-crumb mixture to your cooked string beans and place in a pyrex dish. Pour a small water glass of sour cream over the top and set into moderate oven to bake for 15 minutes. This is not only delicious with any plain roasted or broiled meat or bird, but a delightful texture-contrast eaten with a vegetable platter or plain boiled vegetables and broiled mushrooms.

MEXICAN SALAD

WILLIAM DOOLEY

  1 *pound ground beef*
  ¼ *cup chopped onion*
  2 *cups (1 pound can) kidney beans, drained*
  ¼ *cup vinegar and oil salad dressing*
  ¼ *cup water*
  1 *tablespoon chili powder*
    salt and pepper
    crushed red pepper and/or tabasco to taste
  1 *medium head iceberg lettuce, finely sliced*
12 *sliced scallions*
  8 *oz. extra sharp cheddar cheese, grated*

Brown meat and onion in salad dressing. Stir in beans, water and seasonings. Simmer 15 minutes.

Combine lettuce, scallions and cheese in large salad bowl. Add meat sauce, toss lightly and serve immediately with tortilla or taco chips.

Serves two to four.

HOT ENDIVE SALAD

KENNETH RIEGEL

1 head of endive or 4 cups of dandelion greens
½ pound of bacon, copped in small bits
2 eggs
  pinch of salt
2 hard-boiled eggs
3 tablespoons flour
4 tablespoons sugar
½ cup of vinegar
2½ cups water

Wash endive and chop in bits. Chop bacon and fry until crisp. Mix eggs, sugar, salt, and flour to a batter; add vinegar and water until well blended. Add to bacon and drippings, cook sauce until thickened. Pour hot mixture over endive and mix together lightly. Garnish with sliced hard-boiled eggs and parsley.

  Serves eight.

GREEK SALAD

SPIRO MALAS

3 *juicy tomatoes, sliced*
½ *pound Feta cheese, crumbled*
½ *raw onion, sliced, (more, if you like onion)*
   and sprinkled with oregano
   olive oil and wine vinegar, to your liking

Mix all ingredients and serve at room temperature.

Most Greek salads have too many ingredients and I feel it ruins the taste. Here, you can concentrate on just the few and it is delicious.

POTATO KUGEL

JAN PEERCE

1 *pound potatoes*
1 *egg*
¼ *teaspoon baking powder*
2 *tablespoons melted chicken fat or shortening*
   season to taste

Grate potatoes on medium sized grate into a bowl of cold water. Wash grated potatoes until snowy white. Strain thoroughly. Mix into a bowl with remaining ingredients. Put into greased popover pan and bake at 325° for about 45 minutes or until golden brown and a toothpick will come out clean.

RUSSIAN OR ORIENTAL EGGPLANT

JAN PEERCE

1 *medium sized eggplant*
   three medium onions
   oil
2-3 *tablespoons of chili sauce*
   salt and pepper

Put whole eggplant in shallow baking pan in 350° oven for ½ hour, or until browned. Cook three onions in oil until golden brown, do not fry. When ready, add 2 to 3 tablespoons of chili sauce to onions and oil. If desired, mince one clove of garlic into onions. Peel eggplant while still warm and strain through a sieve. Mix chili, onion, oil mixture and put this through a food grinder. Season to taste with salt and pepper and then simmer mixture for an additional 10 minutes. Cool and serve.

FLORIAN FRUIT SALAD DRESSING

KEN MALUCELLI

½ *cup mayonnaise*
½ *cup sour cream*
½ *cup natural yogurt*
1 *tablespoon lemon or lime juice*
1 *teaspoon cider or white vinegar*
½ *teaspoon dill weed*
¼ *teaspoon mint flakes*
   a pinch of nutmeg
   salt and pepper to taste
   paprika

Mix all ingredients together. Sprinkle with paprika on served portions. This is an excellent bright, creamy dressing for fruit salads or avocado, tomato, or lettuce salads.

BEET AND ENDIVE SALAD

JOHN REARDON

3 *small Belgian endive heads*
1 *16 ounce can sliced beets*
½ *bunch watercress*
2 *tablespoons lemon juice or white wine vin-*
  egar
  salt and pepper to taste
2 *tablespoons olive oil*

With a sharp, knife, cut endive crosswise in ½ inch sections. Separate leaves, wash and drain thoroughly. Place in a bowl. Remove hard stems from watercress and chop. Drain beets and cut slices in half. Add to endive. Whisk together oil, lemon juice (or vinegar), salt and pepper, and pour over salad and toss lightly.

Serves four.

CAESAR SALAD

BRUCE YARNELL
JOAN PATENAUDE

1 *clove garlic*
½ *cup olive oil*
1 *egg*
2 *tablespoons fresh lemon juice*
½ *cup grated parmesan*
1 *teaspoon Worcestershire sauce*
5 *anchovy fillets (skip this, if served with a spicy dish)*
handful of parsley
½ *teaspoon salt*
¼ *teaspoon pepper*
¼ *cup crumbled blue cheese*
1 *teaspoon wheat germ*
1 *large head Romaine lettuce*
croutons

Blend all ingredients but the lettuce and croutons, for 10 seconds. Place bite-size lettuce leaves into a wooden bowl. (Very often I add a few rings of Spanish onion). Pour over dressing and add the croutons.

AMISH CABBAGE WITH SOUR CREAM AND BACON

KENNETH RIEGEL

  1 *head cabbage, sliced*
  ½ *pound sliced bacon*
  2 *tablespoons flour*
  2 *large potatoes, peeled and thickly sliced*
     salt and freshly ground pepper
  ½ *pint cultured sour cream*
     dash of cider vinegar
1¾ *cups boiling water*
  2 *small chopped carrots*

Fry bacon until crisp, drain and pour nearly all of the fat out of the pan. Set aside bacon. In the remaining fat mix cabbage, carrots and potatoes, sprinkle with flour, add the water, salt and pepper, vinegar, and cover. Cook slowly for 50 minutes. When ready to serve, place cabbage and potatoes into a casserole and top with sour cream and crumbled bacon.

Serves 6.

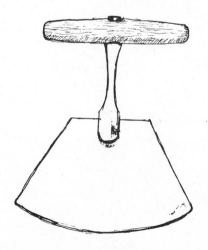

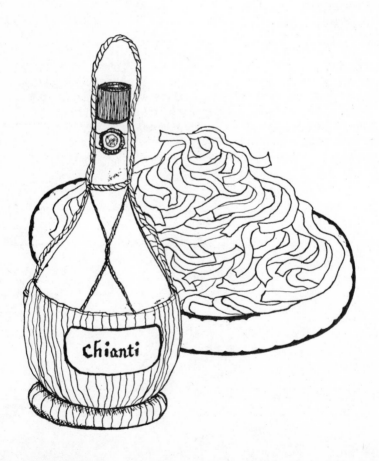

Rice & Pasta Dishes

PERSIAN RICE WITH ALMONDS

JUDITH BLEGEN

6 *cups cooked rice*
1 *large raw potato, peeled and cut into slices*
  ¼ inch thick
2 *large onions, sliced thin*
½ *cup blanched almonds*
½ *cup white raisins*
¼ *pound butter*

Place the cooked rice in a colander, cover it, and steam the rice over a small amount of boiling water for about an hour. This separates and fluffs the grains of rice. Cover the bottom of the heaviest cooking pot you have with the slices of raw potato. A heavy iron pot is best if you have one. Be sure that the entire bottom is covered as the potatoes on the bottom of the pot keep the rice from burning. Alternate layers of the rice, onions, almonds, and raisins. Dot each layer with bits of butter as you go along. Use up all the ingredients in this manner. Place a heavy lid on the pot. Judith suggests wrapping the lid, inverted, in a dish towel and weighting it down with a heavy object. This helps to create steam and it is the long, slow steaming that makes this dish so good. Let the rice steam for at least 1 hour; but it can cook for as long as 2 hours, as the layer of potatoes will keep the rice from scorching. The mingling of all these good ingredients creates a tantalizing flavor, and the Persian rice is an attractive dish to serve on special occasions.

Serves six to eight.

ITALIAN DELIGHT

DONNA PETERSEN

1 *medium onion, chopped*
1 *pound ground beef*
1 *can creamed corn*
1 *8-oz. can tomato sauce*
1 *small can sliced olives*
1 *teaspoon salt*
1 *teaspoon chili powder*
6 *oz. egg noodles*
  grated cheese, if desired

Brown onion in oil until tender in a large frying pan; add meat and brown thoroughly. Add the corn, tomato sauce and sliced olives, rinsing out the cans with small amounts of warm water for added moisture. Add seasonings, then noodles which have been boiled in salted water. Place in a large casserole, top with grated cheese, if desired, and bake uncovered in a 350° oven for approximately 45 minutes, or until casserole is brown and bubbling.

SPAGHETTI ALLA CAPOBIANCO

TITO CAPOBIANCO

1 *pound spaghetti #3*
2 *garlic cloves (peeled)*
2 *green olives pitted*
2 *black olives pitted*
3 *tablespoon capers*
1 *bar butter (¼ pound)*
1 *can of boneless anchovies in oil*
½ *cup olive oil*

Chop garlic, olives and anchovies. Mix them with capers and add melted butter. Keep mix warm.

Boil spaghetti in salted water for 18 minutes. Strain pasta; mix it in a bowl with the olive oil. Serve with 2 tablespoons of mix with each serving. Add grated cheese to your taste.

You can keep leftover mix in refrigerator for 2 weeks if you like.

BULGHOUR PILAF

ARA BERBERIAN

1 *cup cracked wheat*
½ *cup vermicelli noodles*
⅛ *pound butter*
2 *cups chicken broth*
salt to taste

Melt the butter in a shallow pan. Break up vermicelli into pieces and fry in the butter until slightly browned, stirring constantly.

Wash and drain the cracked wheat well, then add it to the vermicelli. Saute them together for a few minutes, always stirring. Then add the boiling broth, cover and cook on a low fire for 20 minutes or until all the liquid is absorbed. Take the pan off the fire and, keeping it covered, let it sit 15-20 minutes before serving. Make sure the pilaf is warm and stir it once well.

Serves four.

LINGUINE WITH WHITE CLAM SAUCE

STEPHANIE VON BUCHAU

½ *pound linguine*
8 *cloves garlic - minced*
¼ *stick butter*
¼ *cup olive oil*
1 *tablespoon parsley*
1 *tablespoon sweet basil*
1 *can clams*
 pepper (fresh ground)
1 *cup dry white wine*

While cooking linguine al dente, prepare sauce as follows. Sizzle minced garlic in butter and olive oil (oil keeps butter from burning). When garlic is soft—do not let it get brown—add parsley and sweet basil. Add one can whole clams with about half their juice. Heat thoroughly. Add fresh ground pepper to taste. At the last minute add wine. Heat and serve immediately on piping hot linguine.

NOTE: You can also use this sauce on spaghetti, but it works best on the thinner varieties such as spaghettini or vermicelli.
 Serves two.

PASTA ALLA TITO GOBBI

TITO GOBBI

 3 *large red tomatoes*
 1 *celery stalk*
 1 *small carrot*
 3 *tablespoons olive oil*
 1 *pound or 1 box #9 Spaghetti*
   a sprinkle of garlic powder
15 *leaves of fresh basil or 2 tbsp. dried basil*
   salt and pepper

Peel and slice the tomatoes (round). Chop the celery and the carrot in very small pieces. Place tomatoes, celery and carrots in a large dutch oven, add to this mixture three tablespoons of olive oil, a sprinkle of garlic powder. Put the dish in to a 250° oven while spaghetti or linguine is cooking. When your pasta is al dente drain completely. Take the dish from the oven and put the pasta on top carefully mixing everything together with the basil and, if needed, add a few drops of olive oil.

Serve immediately and "Buon appetito" con la pasta alla Tito Gobbi.

SPAGHETTI ALLA MATRICIANA

JOSHUA HECHT

1 *pound bacon (thick sliced)*
1 *large onion*
½ *cup fresh chopped parsley*
3 *large cloves of garlic*
1 *two-pound can Italian peeled tomatoes*
  olive oil (barely enough to cover a large frying pan)
  peperoncino (hot peppers) just one large pinch
  Parmesan cheese grated
  box of thin Italian spaghetti

Fry all the bacon until almost crisp and drain on paper towels. Discard bacon grease. Coat clean frying-pan with olive oil and place on medium-small fire. Combine onion, which you have diced, with peperoncino. Put garlic through press and mix with onion and peperoncino. Add to pan and fry until nicely browned, stirring frequently. Add entire can of tomatoes, mix well and lower flame a bit. (Make sure mixture continues to bubble). Let simmer for five minutes and then add bacon which you have crumbled or torn into *small* pieces. Mix well and simmer until mixture thickens slightly. (This means that the tomato liquid will have partially cooked away). Prepare spaghetti "al dente" and, just before serving, add freshly chopped parsley to mixture, stirring it in. Bring spaghetti and sauce to table and serve. Sprinkle on a bit of grated Parmesan, and "eccola!"—you are dining with the Hechts in Roma. "Buon appetito".

RISOTTO MILANESE

LICIA ALBANESE

2½ cups of rice (uncooked)
5 tablespoons of butter
5 tablespoons olive oil
2 tablespoons chopped beef marrow (optional)
3 small onions chopped
2 cups grated Parmesan cheese
½ pound sliced mushrooms (optional)
2 cloves garlic, chopped and mashed (optional)
2½ quarts chicken broth or stock
a pinch of saffron
¼ cup Madera or dry white wine

Melt the butter in a heavy saucepan, add the olive oil and the beef marrow. Add the chopped onions and the garlic, if you are using it. Saute until the onions are pale gold.. Stir in the raw rice (preferably Avorio-Italian) and cook over moderate heat for five minutes, stirring constantly. Add the chicken stock which has been previously boiled, about a cup at a time. As the rice absorbs the liquid add the next cup, stirring frequently. Dilute the saffron with a little chicken stock and add to the rice. The rice should cook covered for at least 15 minutes, until all the liquid has been absorbed. If desired, add a half pound of sliced mushrooms before covering the rice. Before serving, lightly stir in the cheese and a few small lumps of butter.

CANNELLONI

ANNA MOFFO

    butter and olive oil
2 *8–ounce cans peeled tomatoes*
1 *small onion, chopped*
2 *tablespoons tomato paste*
1 *bunch chopped parsley*
2 *cloves chopped garlic*
1 *tablespoon garlic juice*
12 *eggs*
1 *pound top of round, ground*
1 *pound mushrooms, chopped*
1 *pound grated Parmesan cheese*
½ *cup concentrated beef broth*
½ *cup concentrated chicken broth*
½ *pound butter*
1 *cup flour*
1 *quart hot milk*

In a little butter and olive oil, saute the onion, garlic and parsley. Add the tomatoes and tomato paste with a sprinkling each of basil and thyme. Let cook for an hour. While the sauce is cooking, saute the mushrooms in olive oil with the garlic juice. Make very small meatballs out of the ground round, and fry them in the same pan, after removing the mushrooms. When the meatballs are done (not too well done), return the mushrooms to the pan. When the sauce has finished cooking, mix in the meat and mushroom mixture. The total should have a peanut butter consistency. Meanwhile, make the cannelloni (crepes). Use a six-inch teflon frying pan. Beat the eggs with salt and pepper, diluting with some of the broth so that they are not too thick. Cover the bottom of the pan with olive oil and let it get hot. Put a tablespoon of the egg mixture in the hot oil. It should cover the bottom of the pan thinly. Keep moving the pan until no liquid runs off. Slide crepe onto paper towel. Repeat the process until all the mixture is used. Should make about two dozen crepes.

    Grease a rectangular baking dish with butter. Fill the crepes with the mixture, using two tablespoons in the center of each. Be sure to leave room at the edges, so that in folding them, none of the filling will run out. Fold and place in the baking dish.

In a sauce pan, melt ¼ pound of butter. Add the cup of flour and cook until it is absorbed and the mixture becomes a beige color. Gradually stir in the hot milk. Spoon over the crepes, sprinkle with Parmesan cheese and bake for 30 minutes at 325°.

Serves eight.

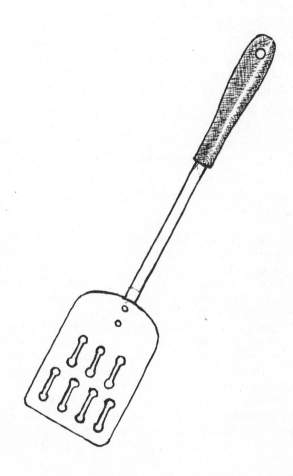

FISH SAUCE LASAGNA

HENRY MC GUCKIN

This sauce is better when prepared the day before it is used.

3-4 cloves of chopped garlic
2 tablespoons chopped fresh parsley
¼-½ chopped green pepper
a few sliced green olives (optional)
sliced fresh mushrooms (optional)
1 can flat anchovies, cut up (reserve oil)
1 can tuna, crumbled
2 cans tomato paste
1 28 oz. can tomatoes
¼ cup red wine
a pinch Italian seasoning
1 box lasagna noodles
grated Parmesan cheese

In a heavy skillet, heat oil from anchovies or small amount of olive oil. Saute garlic and parsley over moderate heat. Do not brown. Add green peppers, then the olives and mushrooms if they are used. Saute for a few seconds, then add anchovies and tuna. Stir well and cook a few seconds more. Add tomato paste, blending all ingredients thoroughly. Add the tomatoes, breaking them in small pieces. Add wine and about half of the tomatoes' liquid. Stir well. Add Italian seasoning. Cover and simmer for about 1 hour, stirring once in a while. If mixture seems too liquid at the end of the cooking period, uncover and reduce at medium heat for a few minutes.

Cook lasagna according to directions on the package. Drain. In a buttered pyrex dish, 12x8, arrange layers of lasagna, sauce, Parmesan cheese, ending with sauce then cheese. Bake uncovered at 350° for ½ hour. Serve with garlic bread and a tossed green salad.

Serves six.

EGG NOODLES ALLA BOLOGNESE

EZIO FLAGELLO

1 *pound egg noodles*
1 *large onion*
1 *small can mushrooms*
1 *bell pepper, cut in 1" strips*
3 *slices ham*
1 *tablespoon diced celery*
1¼ *cups water*
1 *teaspoon tomato paste*
  salt and pepper to taste
1 *pound chopped meat*
2 *tablespoons vegetable oil*
1 *tablespoon carrot shirrings*
⅛ *teaspoon garlic powder*
1 *tablespoon chopped parsley*
⅛ *teaspoon marjoram*
⅛ *teaspoon basil leaf (dried)*
1 *cup white wine*
  grated cheese

Brown meat, onion, carrot, celery, bell pepper in two tablespoons of oil. Add water, ham, garlic powder, parsley, marjoram, and basil. Cook slowly, until water evaporates. Add tomato paste, salt, pepper, mushrooms, and wine. Cook for one hour. Pour bolognese sauce over 1 pound cooked egg noodles, and serve. Add grated cheese, if desired.

Serves five.

This recipe from his forthcoming book *"There's a Basso in the Kitchen"*

LINGUINE ALLA LICIA ALBANESE

LICIA ALBANESE

1 *eight oz. package linguine or spaghetti
20% Protein Linguine, cooked according to
package directions
lemon wedges*
1 *pint heavy sour cream, warmed in double
boiler*
1 *four oz. jar black caviar*

Combine linguine and warm sour cream. Sprinkle caviar over top
and serve with lemon wedges.

Serves two.

****

Giovanni Buitoni, the septuagenarian head of the Buitoni-
Perugina food empire, became a professional opera singer in
just one unique performance. This event took place at Carnegie
Hall on November 27, 1961. With flash bulbs popping and news-
reel cameras rolling, the seventy-year old pasta king sang the
duet "La ci darem la mano", from DON GIOVANNI, with the Met's
Licia Albanese as his partner. They have been friends for years
and it was only natural that he ask her to share the stage with him
for his Carnegie Hall debut.

The Buitonis and the singer, with her husband Joseph Gimma,
dine together frequently, and Giovanni is continually surprising
Licia with some new pasta preparation. Especially for her he
created this dish, an extravagant offering of pasta swirled in sour
cream and garnished with black caviar.

MALTAGLIATI CON FAGIOLI

LUCIANO PAVAROTTI

3 tablespoons oil
½ cup chopped onions
½ cup chopped carrots
2½ quarts water
2 beef bouillon cubes
1 cup tagliatelle (broken into 2-inch pieces)
3.3 ounces (1/3 cup) margarine or butter
½ cup chopped celery
1 large can red Italian tomatoes
  pinch of salt and pepper
2 cups boiled beans (white)
  grated Parmesan

Melt the butter and oil in a dutch oven or heavy pan. When it is very hot, add the celery, carrots and onion and saute until tender but not brown. Then add the can of tomatoes and the water. Add the salt and pepper to taste and the bouillon cubes. Boil for 10 minutes. Then add the boiled beans and cook for ½ hour over low heat. Add the pasta and cook for another 10 minutes and serve with the finest grated Parmesan.

Serves four.

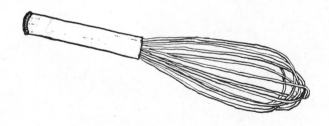

Main Dishes

ROAST PORK LOIN AND RED CABBAGE

RICHARD MUNDT

5 *pound center piece pork loin*
red cabbage
prunes and apples

Cut a slit along the bones leaving a small opening in pork loin into which pre-soaked prunes and apple wedges are to be placed. Salt the pork well, tie up and bake for 2½ hours at 350° with a little water in the pan. Baste often and use the juices for gravy.

The red cabbage should be shredded fine. In a deep pot, make a marinade of vinegar, sugar and a little water. Add ⅛ pound of butter and allow cabbage to steam in this mixture at least 2½ to 3 hours, turning mixture once in a while.

Serve with mashed sweet potatoes.

PEPPER STEAK

CESARE CURZI

1¾ *pounds sirloin steak*
1 *cup Cointreau*
1 *cup brandy*
3 *tablespoons whole peppercorns*
¼ *stick clarified butter*

Marinate the steak which has been cut to ½ inch thickness in the liquor. Break three tablespoons of peppercorns with a hammer in a separate cloth. Spread the cracked pepper on the steak, rubbing the spice into the meat. Saute the steak over hot fire quickly in clarified butter.

SNITZ AND KNEPP

KENNETH RIEGEL

2-4 *pounds of cured smoked ham*
  4 *cups of apple snitz (Sweet dried)*
  3 *tablespoons brown sugar*
  2 *cups apple cider*

Wash dried apples, cover with water and soak overnight. In morning, cover ham with water and cook slowly for 3 hours. Add apples and water and cider to ham. Add brown sugar and cook 1 hour longer.

DUMPLINGS (KNEPP)

  4 *eggs*
  1 *cup flour*
2½ *teaspoons baking powder*
    salt

Sift together dry ingredients. Stir in beaten eggs. Add a little milk if too stiff (so that it drips from the spoon.) Should make eight dumplings. Drop the dumplings into boiling ham and apples. Cover pot tightly and cook 10 to 12 minutes. Do not lift cover until ready to serve. Serve directly from cooking pot—piping hot.
  Serves eight.

WELSH CHEESE PUDDING

DELME BRYN-JONES

4 *slices of bread*
some good Welsh farm butter (sweet butter)
1 *pint of creamy milk*
1 *pound grated Caerphilly cheese*
1 *egg*
salt and pepper
tabasco

Toast the bread on one side only, and butter the untoasted side. Lay two pieces, toasted side down in a dish and sprinkle the cheese and seasoning over them. Sandwich the remaining slices, buttered side down, on top and sprinkle with some of the cheese. Bring the milk to the boil, allow to cool and add the egg, well beaten into it. Pour this over the sandwich, let it stand for 20 minutes or so and then bake it for 20 minutes in a moderate oven. If you like tabasco, as I do, whisk a few drops into the milk before adding to the bread. This makes a very pleasant light luncheon or supper dish.
Serves two.

VEAL CUTLETS IN PORT

CHESTER LUDGIN

1½ *pounds veal cutlets*
1 *onion diced*
3 *tablespoons butter*
¾ *cup of port wine*
  juice of ½ lemon
1 *cup cream*
  dash of cayenne pepper
⅛ *teaspoon of thyme*

Brown veal and onion in butter. Cover. Simmer until lightly browned and tender. Remove meat. Keep warm. Add remaining ingredients to drippings. Heat, stirring, but do not boil. Serve over meat.

Serves four to six.

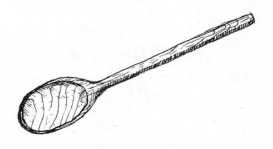

BEEFSTEAK WORONOFF

EVELYN LEAR

4 half-pound slices of filet of beef
½ pound butter
½ teaspoon rosemary or tarragon
   salt and pepper

SAUCE:

1/3 teaspoon mustard (Dijon)
2 teaspoons Worcestershire sauce
2 tablespoons cognac

Combine the ingredients for the sauce, mixing thoroughly. Heat half the butter in the skillet and add the beef slices and rosemary or tarragon. Cook very quickly over high heat. Two minutes for each side is sufficient. Season to taste, add the balance of the butter and the sauce, and continue to cook for 2 minutes more, no longer. Turn the meat once during the cooking and serve with sauce, slightly reduced and strained.
   Serves four.

FILET OF SOLE

LORENZO ALVARY

2 pounds filet of sole
1 small bottle of clam juice
1 large onion
1 tablespoon vegetable oil
3 tablespoons butter
   tarragon, salt, and pepper
1 tablespoon vermouth

Cook chopped onion slowly in oil. Cover bottom of flat glass pyrex dish with onion. Fold filets. Place in onion base. Dot with butter. Pour clam juice over fish. Season to taste with tarragon and salt. Bring to boil on top of stove. When partially cooked, cover dish with aluminum foil. Put in preheated oven at 350°. After 10 minutes add vermouth and sprinkle with grated cheese. Brown under broiler.

Serve with dry toast. Raw zucchini with dill vinegar is an excellent condiment.

SMOTHERED STEAK ROLL-UPS

WILLIAM HARNESS

1½ *pounds thinly sliced round steak (¼ inch thick)*
1½ *cups prepared packaged herb seasoned stuffing*
½ *cup water*
2 *tablespoons shortening*
1 *can (10½ oz.) condensed consomme, cream of vegetable, mushroom or golden mushroom soup (the latter is my favorite)*

Cut steak into 6 pieces (about 8 inches by 4 inches). Pound with meat hammer or edge of heavy skillet. Place ¼ cup stuffing near center of each piece of meat. Roll up. Tuck in ends and fasten with skewers or toothpicks. In skillet, brown roll-ups in shortening then pour off fat. Add soup and water. Cover, cook over low heat for 1¼ hours or until tender. Stir now and then.
  Serves 6.

Variation. Put onion slice and ½ piece bacon in middle of thinly sliced steak and cook as above.

OXTAIL IN WINE

ARCHIE DRAKE

3½ *pounds fresh oxtails, large segments*
  1 *large onion*
  2 *large bay leaves*
  1 *large pinch rosemary*
    ground allspice
    salt and pepper
  1 *large cup Burgundy (Charles Krug or Mondavi are especially good)*

Line medium roasting pan with roasting wrap. Slice onion in layers on the bottom of the pan; crumble bay leaf and rosemary over the onion. Place oxtails in single layer over onion and spices. Salt and pepper to taste and add wine. Finally, sprinkle ground allspice sparingly but evenly over all. Close wrap tightly and roast in a slow oven (250°-300°) for 3½ hours.

After serving cooked oxtail, place liquid in refrigerator for 24 hours. Remove the layer of fat that will form on the top. What is left is a firm pure beef gelatin which can be used in stock, in soups or stews, or is delicious cold served with toast or crackers as an appetizer.

Serves four.

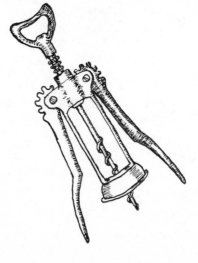

SALT'INBOCCA A LA MOSLI

ROBERT MOSLEY

1 *pound veal cutlets cut for scallopine*
¼ *pound prosciutto*
¼ *pound Swiss cheese*
½ *cup Parmesan cheese*
2 *cloves garlic*
½ *cup fresh parsley*
5 *tablespoons butter*
  salt and pepper to taste
¼ *cup Sauterne*

Place each piece of veal on sheet of paper towel. Chop parsley and garlic together and sprinkle them generously over veal. Place prosciutto and Swiss cheese cut in small strips on top of veal. Sprinkle with Parmesan cheese. Add seasoning. In frying pan melt butter. Roll the veal and fasten with toothpicks. When butter is hot, place the veal in pan and cook over medium flame shaking pan gently, until veal browns. Add ¼ cup white Sauterne wine and cook another three minutes. Serve with broccoli au gratin or buttered yellow squash and green zucchini.

CHICKEN IN THE POT

JAN PEERCE

6 *pounds fowl*
6 to 8 *chicken feet, scaled, skinned, nails removed*
6 *quarts water*
1½ *tablespoons salt*
4 *stalks celery*
½ *celery root*
1 *parsnip*
2 *medium sized onions*
3 *medium sized carrots*
½ *teaspoon pepper*

Select an older fowl; ask the butcher for extra chicken feet. Singe, clean and disjoint the chicken. Put in large pot and cover with boiling water. Add vegetables. Bring to a boil and allow to simmer for 3 hours. Remove chicken when tender. After soup has cooked for 3 hours, strain, remove fat and season to taste. Serve chicken in casserole with Matzo Balls and soup. The carrots may be sliced and added to the casserole as a vegetable. Heat in casserole and serve thoroughly hot.

Serves six to eight.

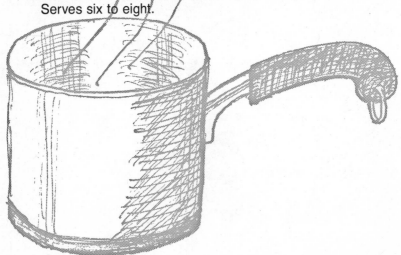

SZEGEDI GULYAS

JULIA EMOED-WALLACE

  4 *strips of lean bacon*
  1 *pound beef, cubed*
  1 *pound pork, cubed*
1½ *pounds chopped onions*
1½ *pounds sauerkraut*
  3 *tablespoons Hungarian paprika*
  4 *cloves crushed garlic*
    salt to taste
  1 *pint sour cream*
    peppercorns
    juniper berries
    carraway seeds

Cut lean bacon into small pieces and melt in large pot. Add onions and stir until golden. Add cubed pork and beef slowly, letting it set until very slightly browned. Add seasonings and then add sauerkraut quickly, not letting paprika burn. Stir mixture then put the lid on the pot and let simmer for at least an hour or more until meat is very tender. Add sour cream 10 minutes before serving. This tastes best when it has been warmed up several times. Serve with extra sour cream. This dish tastes very good with Spaetzle or Hungarian "Nockesh."

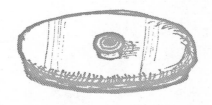

CHICKEN & LOBSTER CANTONESE

ELEANOR STEBER

1½ cups (12 oz.) leftover turkey or chicken
1 6½ oz. can lobster, drained
1 tablespoon safflower oil
1 clove garlic, minced (optional)
1 green pepper, cut in strips
1 small onion, sliced
1 cup celery, diced
  pepper
½ cup boiling water
1 chicken bouillon cube
½ cup (small can) water chestnuts, drained and
  sliced
2 cups bean sprouts, drained
2 tablespoons soy sauce
½ teaspoon ginger

Heat oil in skillet (or wok), tilting pan to coat bottom. Saute garlic, green pepper, onion, and celery. Dissolve bouillon cube in water, and add. Cover, and simmer 8-10 minutes. Add chicken, lobster, and all remaining ingredients and simmer an additional 5 minutes. If necessary, add a little more water.

Serves six.

I have great pleasure cooking this dish in an electric Chinese wok—also an excellent conversation piece.

CHICKEN SURPRISE

RICHARD CLARK

HERB BUTTER:
- ½ *cup butter*
- ½ *cup margarine*
- 1 *tablespoon chopped parsley*
- 1 *teaspoon dried crushed tarragon*
- ½ *teaspoon salt*
- ½ *teaspoon finely minced garlic*
- ¼ *teaspoon pepper*

Cream together all of the above ingredients.

CHICKEN BREASTS:
Debone 3 whole chicken breasts, and cut in half. Place in a bowl of milk and refrigerate while mixing the herb butter. With flour, salt and pepper, dust the chicken breasts. Fry in either butter or vegetable oil for four minutes on each side. Arrange the chicken on a platter. Meanwhile, melt the herb butter and pour over the chicken, or serve extra in a bowl. Decorate the platter with parsley.

The recipe for herb butter can also be doubled, and one half of it frozen for later use.

Serves six.

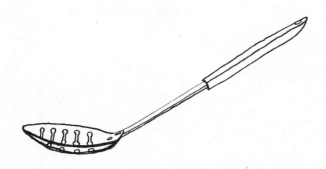

DILL AND PEPPER CURED SALMON

THOMAS STEWART

3 *pounds fresh salmon*
¼ *cup salt*
¼ *cup sugar*
4-5 *teaspoons fresh ground or crushed pepper*
dill stems

SAUCE
5 *tablespoons prepared mustard*
1 *teaspoon powdered mustard*
2-3 *tablespoons sugar*
pinch of salt
white pepper
juice of half a lemon
3 *tablespoons white vinegar*
½ *cup olive oil*
big bunch of fresh dill cut very fine (reserve stems for salmon wrap)

Mix salt, sugar and pepper. Rub into washed and dried salmon. Crush the stems of dill, put on salmon, in between, over and under. Wrap in wax paper and put in deep bowl with a weight on top. Refrigerate for at least sixty hours (2½ days). Turn salmon once a day and pour accumulated fluid over and in between salmon. When ready to serve, remove dill and seasoning. Slice with sharp knife. Serve with creamed spinach or small new potatoes or toast, or all of these! Slice skin, when salmon is done about one inch wide and saute with a little oil and butter in hot frying pan till crisp. Serve with sauce.

To prepare sauce: Mix mustard, sugar, pinch of salt and white pepper. Add juice of lemon and white vinegar. Stir well—drop in olive oil a little at a time while stirring. Add the fresh cut dill. Stir and taste. Add whatever you think is missing—perhaps a little more sugar, more mustard or salt or lemon juice. It is a matter of taste at this point.

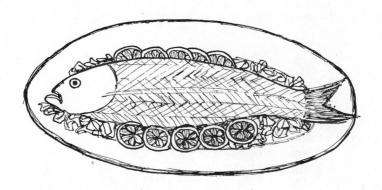

LAMB FILLED RAVIOLI
POLISH-LITHUANIAN STYLE

TERESA ZYLIS-GARA

FILLING

- 2-3 *yellow onions-chopped*
- 1 *pound minced lamb (already cooked and cooled)*
- ¼ *cup water*
- 2 *tablespoons oil*
- 2 *tablespoons butter*
- 5 *sprigs chopped dill*
- ½ *teaspoon salt*
- ½ *teaspoon fresh ground pepper*

RAVIOLI PASTE

- ½ *pound light flour*
- ½ *teaspoon salt*
- 2 *tablespoons butter*
- 1 *egg*
- *salted boiling water*
- *melted butter*

Saute the onions in two tablespoons of oil and two tablespoons butter until golden. Mix with the minced lamb adding the ¼ cup water, dill, pepper and ½ teaspoon salt. Set aside.

Make the ravioli paste by mixing the flour and ½ teaspoon salt and knead in the two tablespoons butter. Add the egg, which has been well beaten and a small amount of milk or water to make a stiff paste. Roll dough out on floured surface—quite thin and cut into 3-4 inch rounds. Put some of the filling on each round, fold over and seal the edges. Put each ravioli carefully into simmering salted water and let them boil for a few minutes till they float to the top. Then remove and put them into another pan where you have kept the melted butter warm. Will keep in a warm oven until ready to serve.

Serves four.

POLLO A LO AGRIDULCE

CAROLE BOGARD

1 tablespoon finely chopped garlic
1 teaspoon crumbled oregano
1 teaspoon salt
½ teaspoon black pepper
6 tablespoons olive oil
1 tablespoon plus ½ cup malt vinegar (white or cider)
1 3½ to 4 pound chicken, cut into serving pieces
1 pound pork sausage
4 to 6 oz.. Canadian bacon, cubed
1 cup chicken stock
½ cup dark-brown sugar
1 teaspoon arrowroot combined with 2 tablespoons cold water

Mash garlic, oregano, salt, and pepper together. Stir in 4 tablespoons of the olive oil and 1 tablespoon of vinegar. Coat the chicken with this mixture. Cover and refrigerate overnight. Brown the sausages and cubed bacon. Drain off the fat. Set aside. Cut up the sausages into ¼ inch slices. In a heavy skillet heat remaining 2 tablespoons oil. Pat the chicken dry and brown it starting skin side down a few pieces at a time. (Discard the marinade.) As they brown transfer them to a plate. Drain off fat. Add chicken stock. Bring to a boil and scrape in any brown particles clinging to the bottom of the skillet. Stir in the brown sugar and vinegar. Return the chicken, sausage and bacon. Cover and simmer 30 minutes. Place chicken, sausage and bacon pieces on a platter. Blend arrowroot into the cooking liquid stirring constantly until thickened. Pour sauce over the chicken. Serve at once.

Serves four.

BEEF BOURGUIGNON

BRUCE YARNELL
JOAN PATENAUDE

4 *tablespoons butter*
3 *pounds round steak, cut into ¾ cubes*
1 *crushed garlic clove*
3 *sliced onions*
4 *tablespoons flour*
2 *cups red Burgundy wine*
1 *cup water*
2 *teaspoons salt*
½ *teaspoon pepper*
½ *teaspoon marjoram*
¼ *teaspoon oregano*
½ *cup strong coffee*

Melt butter in deep frying pan. Add cubed steak, brown all over. Add garlic and onions until onions are soft, *not brown*. Remove meat and onions from pan. Blend flour with remaining butter left in the pan. Add wine, water, seasonings and coffee. Stir until slightly thickened. Return meat and onions to pan. Cover. Bring to a boil. Simmer 1½ hours or until meat is tender. Serve with parslied, buttered broad noodles.

Serves six.

CHICKEN BOMBAY

BIANCA SAROYA

1 *chicken cut in pieces*
½ *cup butter*
1 *onion chopped*
1 *clove garlic crushed*
½ *leaf of thyme*
½ *cup currants*
1 *teaspoon salt*
¼ *teaspoon pepper*
1 *green pepper chopped*
2 *teaspoons curry powder*
1 *large can Italian stewed tomatoes*
  slivered almonds and sherry

Saute the onion and the chicken in a casserole until they are brown. Add green pepper, garlic, curry powder, stewed tomatoes and currants. Season with salt, pepper and sherry to taste. Bake uncovered in a 350° oven for 45 minutes or until chicken is tender. Sprinkle with slivered almonds before serving.

Serves four.

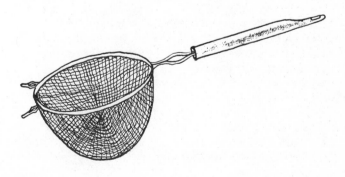

CRABMEAT CASSEROLE

BETTY ALLEN

1 *pound fresh lump crabmeat or 3 packages frozen Alaska King Crab*
1 *pound mushrooms (caps only)*
¼ *cup butter*
2 *tablespoons flour*
1 *cup milk, scalded*
1 *tablespoon fresh chopped parsley*
1 *teaspoon salt (Kosher or Sea Salt)*
1 *teaspoon prepared mustard*
½ *teaspoon horseradish*
2 *scallions, finely chopped*
2 *teaspoons lemon juice*
  dash tabasco
2 *egg yolks*
½ *cup mayonnaise*
½ *cup heavy cream*
1 *teaspoon Worcestershire*

Heat oven to 400° F. Melt ¼ cup butter over low heat, stirring flour slowly. Add horseradish, mustard, parsley, lemon juice and salt. Slowly stir in scalded milk. Cook, stirring to avoid lumpiness until thick. Set aside and cool. Saute mushrooms (which have been sliced) in 1 teaspoon butter, adding salt and pepper to taste. A small squirt of lemon juice brings out the flavor. Add scallions to sauce pan and saute lightly. Add mushrooms and scallions to the cream sauce, then beaten egg yolks, heavy cream, mayonnaise, and Worcestershire. Lastly, add crabmeat. Pick well to avoid bits of cartilage. Put in 1¼ quart casserole. Spread ½ cup fresh bread crumbs which have been tossed with 2 teaspoons melted butter over the top. Sprinkle lightly with paprika and bake until brown and bubbly, (approximately 20 minutes).

STANDING ROOM CHICKEN

REBECCA ROBERTS

      1 *fryer - cut up*
    1½ *cups dry white wine*
      ½ *cup sliced mushrooms*
      1 *can cream of celery soup*
      1 *can cream of mushroom soup*
        lots of butter
        paprika
        salt .
        pepper
        parsley
        garlic powder

Saute chicken in a generous amount of butter in a large pan.
While it is cooking, sprinkle top side with a generous amount of
salt, papper, paprika, parsley and enough garlic powder to clear
out the standee in front of you. Be sure to annoint both sides.
When chicken is golden brown, remove from pan and place in
large dish. Into pan, stir well the cans of soup, be sure to capture
the "goodies" in the bottom of the pan. Very slowly, add the
wine, stirring constantly. Add mushrooms and place chicken
back in pan, spooning sauce over it until it appears to be quite
inebriated. Be sure to add any juice that remains in the platter.
Cover and let simmer for 30-45 minutes or until tender.
   Serves four.

Wild rice and tossed salad are good companions and now you'll
have plenty of time to queue up.

DIVINE CRABMEAT CASSEROLE

JAMES HOOPER

1 *13 oz. can of mushroom soup*
2 *large cans of crabmeat*
2 *4½ oz. jars of minced ripe olives*
2 *cups of seasoned stuffing*
1 *large can of evaporated milk*
1 *small package of slivered almonds*
2 *tablespoons of lemon juice*

Heat the mushroom soup and evaporated milk together. Combine these with the other ingredients and place in a buttered casserole. Bake for 30 minutes in a 350° oven. After removing it from the oven, spread the following on top of the casserole:

½ *cup chopped celery*
1 *cup of mayonnaise*
½ *cup chopped green pepper*
½ *cup chopped green onions and tops*

After chopping the greens fine, mix with mayonnaise and spread over the casserole. Return it to oven and bake 15 minutes longer.

Serves six to eight.

TONNO-MARINER'S STYLE

JAMES McCRACKEN

4 *tablespoons olive oil*
1 *clove garlic*
½ *teaspoon oregano*
1 *#2 can whole tomatoes (Italian) with juice*
1 *small can peas*
  salt and pepper
1 *7 ounce can Tonno (tuna) drained*
1 *small can ripe olives, sliced*

Heat the oil in a heavy skillet and cook the slivered garlic until golden brown. Remove garlic and add tomatoes and oregano, cooking over low heat for ½ hour until tomatoes, oregano, garlic and oil form a smooth sauce. Then add peas and flaked tuna and slivers of ripe olives. Try not to break up the tuna. Heat thoroughly and serve over cooked noodles topped with freshly grated Parmesan cheese.

Serves six.

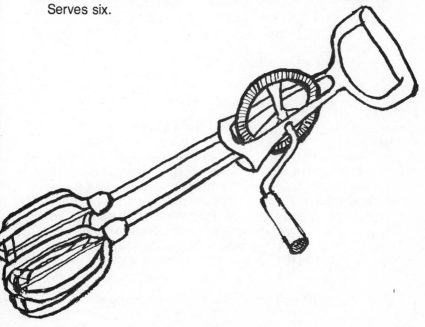

SUKIYAKI ON THE ROAD

SPIRO MALAS

(Travel with electric skillet, a bottle of sake and a bottle of Japanese soy sauce).

- 1 *pound tender beef sliced very thin (or chicken breasts boned, or small meatballs)*
  a piece of suet or 2 tablespoons oil
- ½ *cup sake or dry sherry*
- ½ *cup soy sauce*
- 1 *tablespoon sugar (optional)*

- 2 *onions sliced*
- 1 *bunch scallions cut in 1 inch pieces*
- 1 *bunch radishes*
  Chinese cabbage cut crosswise in one-inch pieces
- 1 *green pepper pared and sliced*
- 10-15 *mushrooms cut in half*
- 1 *bunch watercress without the coarse stems*
- 1 *box frozen peapods thawed*

- 1 *can water chestnuts*   *(if available)*
- 1 *can bamboo shoots*

Heat skillet. Grease it lightly with the suet or oil. Cook the sliced beef quickly. Push it to a corner of the skillet. Add the onions, scallions and radishes, cut in half. Add the sugar. Pour half the sake-soysauce mixture in the skillet. Stir. After a few minutes add the cabbage, pepper and mushrooms. Drain the peapods and add to the skillet. Add water chestnuts and bamboo shoots if you have them. Pour the rest of the sake-soysauce mix into the pan over the vegetables. After a few minutes add the watercress. When it starts to wilt, it is done. Serve piping hot. Make sure you give a little of all the vegetables to each person.

Cold beer goes well with this dish. Serves two generously.

CHICKEN AND PEAR MOUSSE

MARTIAL SINGHER

2½ *cups milk*
4 *packages unflavored gelatin*
2½ *pounds cooked chicken (about 4-5 cups)*
1 *cup mayonnaise*
¼ *cup lemon juice*
1 *teaspoon basil*
2 *cups heavy cream, stiffly beaten*
4 *eggs, separated*
3 *cups chopped pears*
1 *cup chopped onion*
¼ *cup chopped parsley*
2 *teaspoons salt*
½ *teaspoon pepper*

Heat 1½ cups of the milk in the top of a double boiler until a film forms on the surface. In a medium bowl, beat egg yolks until lemon colored and thick. Add heated milk gradually and pour back into the top of the double boiler. Simmer over very low heat, stirring constantly, until custard thickens slightly and coats a spoon. Remove from heat and let cool.

Sprinkle gelatin over 1 cup cold milk to soften (about 2-3 minutes) then dissolve in a saucepan over medium heat. Cool.

Combine in a large bowl custard, gelatin, chicken, pear, onion, mayonnaise, parsley, lemon juice, salt, basil and pepper. Beat egg whites until stiff. Gently fold chicken mixture into beaten cream and egg whites. Fold into a greased 12 cup mold or two 6 cup molds. Chill until firm. Serve with thinly sliced apple and pear wedges (or, if you prefer, crackers—but red apples, with the skin still on, look best, as do nice, firm pears with their skin).

Serves twelve to fourteen.

STUFFED CABBAGE

MAURICE PERESS

1 *large head cabbage*
2 *pounds ground meat (round or chuck)*
1 *egg*
1 *slice white bread soaked in 1 cup warm milk*
3 *large onions chopped and sauted in butter until golden*
1 *cup rice, parboiled*
3 *teaspoons salt*
¼ *teaspoon ground nutmeg*
   fresh ground pepper
½ *pint heavy cream*
   bunch fresh dill

Parboil the rice. Drain and set aside. Chop the onions and saute in butter over low heat. Set aside. Soak bread in milk. Heat cream and add the finely chopped dill. Put meat in large bowl and add rice, onions, bread in milk, egg, salt, nutmeg and pepper. Work thoroughly with a wooden spoon until fluffy and pink. Boil cabbage in large pot for 15 minutes. Drain and let cold water run over cabbage a few minutes. Peel off leaves, one by one. Use scissors to cut out one inch of the coarsest part of the stem. Put a large spoonful of meat on the leaf and fold. Begin with the stem part, then the left and right sides and close with the tip of the leaf. Line them up in a buttered backing pan. Cook in a pre-heated oven 450° for 20 minutes, or until cabbage starts getting browned on top. Lower heat to 350° and baste with one third of the cream with dill. Cook for another 40 minutes basting two more times. When cooked grind fresh pepper over cabbage and let sit for 5 minutes before serving. (Put remaining cabbage cut up a little in one corner of pan and cook with the stuffed cabbage.)
   Serves six.

DOLMADES WITH LEMON SAUCE

SPIRO MALAS

about 50 grapevine leaves
1½ lbs. ground beef (round or chuck)
1 tablespoon salt
2 tablespoon chopped parsley or mint leaf
¾ cup Carolina Rice
½ cup water
2 chopped onions
½ cup butter
fresh ground pepper to taste
5 egg yolks
¾ tablespoon fresh lemon juice

Boil water in a big saucepan. Add vine leaves and leave until softened. Cut off the stem. Drain the leaves bit by bit, as you go along. Saute onions in butter or margarine. Remove frying pan from fire and add meat, salt, pepper, parsley, and uncooked rice. Mix well. Place a big spoonful of mixture on each leaf, shiny side down. Fold over once, then tuck in sides and fold once again. Arrange all close together in a saucepan till they look really crowded, row after row. Place saucer or another saucepan on top of dolmades or they will open up while cooking. Add 1½ cup warm water and cook gently for 1 hour. Make sure water doesn't boil off completely. Add a little if necessary. Beat yolks and add ½ cup cold water, little by little. While beating, add lemon juice. When vine leaves are ready, drain, but save broth. Add to beaten yolks slowly. Put over low heat and stir for 10 minutes. When thickened pour over dolmades and serve.

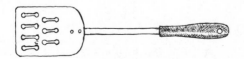

FRESH CRAB DISH

MARTINA ARROYO

1/3 *cup chopped onion*
1/3 *cup chopped green pepper*
1/3 *cup chopped celery*
2 or 3 *sections garlic clove, chopped fine*
    salt and black pepper to taste
    oregano
1 *bouillon cube (chicken or beef)*
1 *tablespoon chopped fresh parsley or dried parsley flakes*
    Tabasco sauce
    hot pepper sauce
1 *pound fresh lump crabmeat*
    grated Parmesan cheese or breadcrumbs

Preheat to 300° enough olive oil to cover the bottom of an electric skillet. Saute slowly, with lid covering, the first four of the above ingredients until cooked through. Add salt, black pepper to taste, and a touch of oregano. Add bouillon cube and parsley. Add to taste (our's is for very hot!) Tabasco sauce and hot pepper sauce. At the last minute, toss the one pound of lump crabmeat, well checked for bones. Toss only long enough for crabmeat to soak up the sauce, then pack into seafood shells. Cover with grated Parmesan cheese, or breadcrumbs, and bake in medium oven until cheese is melted and browned.

Fills five or six large shells or eight to ten appetizer-sized shells.

*Reprinted by permission from the Christian Science Monitor
©1966 The Christian Science Publishing Society
All Rights Reserved*

MOUSSAKA

SPIRO MALAS

3 eggplants
2 pounds ground lamb or beef
2 onions, chopped
1 garlic clove, minced
  cinnamon
  nutmeg
½ teaspoon fines herbes
2 tablespoons parsley
1 can tomato sauce (8 ounce)
½ cup red wine
  olive oil
  butter
  salt and pepper
4 cups bechamel sauce (white sauce)
3 egg yolks (optional)
  grated cheese

Peel and cut the eggplant lengthwise into ½ inch slices; sprinkle with salt, and set aside on paper towels to absorb the moisture. Meanwhile, prepare the meat sauce. Saute the ground meat in butter with salt and pepper, onions and garlic, crumbling the meat with a fork. When the meat is evenly browned, add ¼ teaspoon nutmeg, ¼ teaspoon cinnamon, fines herbes, parsley and tomato sauce; stir to mix well. Add wine and simmer for 20 minutes. Wipe the salted eggplant; lightly oil a skillet with a pastry brush and quickly fry the eggplant over very high heat; lay on paper towels to drain. (By following this method carefully the vegetable will not absorb too much oil). In a greased 9x13x2 inch baking pan, place a layer of eggplant, top with the meat mixture, sprinkle with grated cheese, and cover with bechamel sauce. (Add ¼ teaspoon nutmeg to the bechamel, and for an exceedingly rich sauce, add 3 egg yolks to the sauce after it has cooked). Top the moussaka lavishly with grated cheese and bake at 350° for one hour. Allow to cool, and then cut into 3-inch squares.

Serves twelve.

Variation: 2 pounds zucchini, sliced or 2 pounds potatoes, peeled and fried, may be substituted for the eggplant.

TEMPURA

SHIGEMI MATSUMOTO

1 *large electric skillet, filled to within an inch of the top with vegetable oil*
   Hime Tempura batter mix
1 *pound fresh jumbo shrimp*
1 *bunch asparagus*
½ *pound fresh mushrooms*
½ *pound green beans*
1 *large sweet potato*
   onions–green, white or red (Also may substitute virtually any green vegetable desired, including carrots, parsley, celery, green peppers, broccoli, etc.)

Heat oil to hot. Shell and prepare shrimp by slicing from the back of the shrimp toward the legs so that it will lay flat, and then de-vein. Refrigerate.

Prepare vegetables: cut asparagus into 2 or 3 inch spears; slice fresh mushrooms in half; string green beans; peel sweet potato and slice into ¼ inch thicknesses; slice onions as desired. Mix a cup or more batter as needed—following. Refrigerate.

Dip each ingredient into batter and place carefully into hot oil. Turn shrimp and vegetables gently and cook to desired crispness. Will cook quickly. If desired, place napkin on each dinner plate to absorb oil.

Place shrimp and vegetables on a large platter in an attractive manner, and in the true Japanese style, you may cook and serve your guests at the table.

Serves four.

SHRIMP CREOLE
IN SPINACH-AND-RICE RING

GRACE BUMBRY

1 *small onion, sliced*
2 *parsley sprigs*
½ *lemon, sliced*
2 *teaspoons of salt*
3 *whole black peppercorns*
1½ *pounds shelled, deveined raw shrimp*

CREOLE SAUCE
¼ *cup butter or margarine*
¼ *cup chopped onion*
¼ *cup coarsely chopped green pepper*
1 *teaspoon Worcestershire Sauce*
1 *can (1 pound) tomatoes, undrained*
1 *can (8 oz.) tomato sauce*
1 *teaspoon salt*
1 *bay leaf*

SPINACH-AND-RICE RING
4 *cups cooked rice*
½ *cup finely chopped spinach*
2 *tablespoons butter or margarine, melted*

In a large saucepan, combine 1 quart water, the sliced onion, parsley sprigs, lemon, 2 teaspoons salt, and the black pepper-corns. Bring to boiling, add shrimp. Return to boiling, reduce heat, simmer covered five minutes or just until tender. Drain shrimp; set aside until ready to use. Meanwhile, preheat the oven to 350°. Butter a five cup ring mold. Make Creole Sauce: In a large skillet saute onion and green peppers in butter—about five minutes or until onion is golden. Add Worcestershire Sauce, tomatoes, tomato sauce, salt, pepper and bay leaf; bring to boil-ing. Reduce heat and simmer, uncovered, ten minutes. Remove and discard bay leaf. Add shrimp to sauce; simmer, covered for fifteen minutes or until shrimp is hot. Meanwhile, prepare spinach and rice ring; in large bowl, combine rice, spinach and melted butter; toss until well blended. Pack lightly into mold, smoothing top. Bake ten minutes, or until heated. To serve, run small spatula around edge of mold; invert onto warm serving platter. Fill with shrimp and sauce.

Serves six.

POULET A COUCHET BLANCHE

BLANCHE THEBOM

1 *chicken, cut in pieces*
1 *pound coarse corn bread dressing*
$1/3$ *cup coarse uncooked Kasha*
$1/3$ *cup crushed peanuts*
  salt to taste
  pepper to taste
  crushed rosemary leaves
  dill seed (optional)

Section chicken into desired servings. Thoroughly grease bottom and four sides of a 2 or 3 inch deep roasting pan and lightly pack dressing mix into pan, working into corners. Lay chicken sections on bed of dressing. Add 1 can of milk to 1 can cream of celery soup and pour over chicken. If the flavor of dill is desired, add dill seed to soup mixture before covering chicken. Cover entire pan and contents with heavy foil, seal and bake in medium oven (350°) for 1½ hours. Serve in pan after removing foil and garnishing chicken with slices of red canned pepper or parsley for color.

Serves four.

Great for patio parties—it will hold for hours during the dinner 'preliminaries' or tardy guests. The flavor of the chicken and the dressing (which becomes moist with the soup mix and chicken juices) can only improve. The dressing will have formed a hard under-crust which adds to the flavor. Good also in small baking dishes for individual servings.

ROCK CORNISH GAME HENS WITH CRANBERRY-ORANGE STUFFING

DOUGLAS LAWRENCE

8 *cornish game hens*
2½ *cups boiling water*
2 *teaspoons Beau Monde seasoning*
¼ *cup melted butter*

SAUCE:

giblets and stock
pan drippings
1 *tablespoon arrowroot*
1 *tablespoon water*
1 *teaspoon orange peel*
½ *teaspoon Beau Monde*
salt and pepper
3 *tablespoons Orange Curaçao*

STUFFING:

½ *cup butter*
¾ *cup finely chopped celery and celery leaves*
2 *cups chopped cranberries*
6 *tablespoons sugar*
2 *teaspoons orange rind*
1 *teaspoon salt*
½ *teaspoon ground cinnamon*
1 *teaspoon poultry seasoning*
2 *tablespoons orange juice*
2 *cans (11 oz.) Mandarin oranges, drained*
1 *tablespoon Instant Toasted Onion*
4 *cups cubed raisin bread*

Simmer necks and giblets in boiling water seasoned with Beau Monde. Add liver for last 15 minutes only. Wash and dry birds. Salt cavities. Melt ½ cup butter in frying pan. Add celery; cook only until tender. Add next 8 ingredients and toss lightly with butter and celery. Stuff birds and secure drumsticks and wings. Brush with melted butter. Roast at 400° for 1-1½ hours until tender and well-browned. Turn once during roasting. Remove to warm place. Discard necks; chop giblets. Add stock and giblets to drippings in pan. Add orange peel and Beau Monde. Simmer until drippings are well dissolved in stock. Mix arrowroot with water; add to gravy. Stir until thickened and smooth. Correct seasoning. Just before serving add Curaçao. Spoon over hens, and offer extra gravy in sauce boat at the table.

Serves eight.

CRABMEAT IMPERIAL CASSEROLE

LEONTYNE PRICE

1 *large green pepper, diced*
2 *pimientos, diced*
½ *teaspoon salt*
½ *teaspoon freshly ground white pepper*
1 *tablespoon dry mustard*
3 *tablespoons mayonnaise*
2 *eggs, lightly beaten*
3 *tablespoons sherry*
2 *pounds fresh lump crabmeat (back fin)*
  paprika

Preheat the oven to 350°. Mix the diced pepper and pimientos. Add salt, pepper, mustard, mayonnaise, eggs and two tablespoons of the sherry; mix. Carefully fold the crabmeat into the pepper mixture so as not to break the lumps of crab. Add the remaining tablespoon of sherry and place in a buttered casserole. Coat the top of the casserole with a thin layer of mayonnaise and sprinkle with paprika. Bake for fifteen minutes. Serves six.

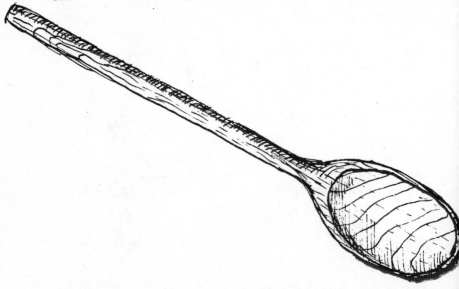

ROAST SNIPE

C. J. Landsdell's recipe for snipe as experienced and recommended by DELME BRYN-JONES.

Snipe, Roast—Some epicures consider a young snipe has been roasted when it has passed through a hot kitchen. Be that as it may, a snipe needs to be roasted rare, and if the oven is hot, 15 minutes will suffice. For those who do not like them rare, 20 minutes at the most will be sufficient for these small birds.

Pluck the birds, do not cut off the head or feet, and do not draw them, for the trail (entrail or intestine) is considered by some a greater delicacy than the bird itself. Truss them as described, in the usual manner, brush all over with melted butter, and set each bird on a slice of buttered toast well spread out in a roasting pan. Have the oven well heated to 450° F. and roast the birds for 15 minutes only if the guests are epicures. If not, roast for 20 minutes. Send to table with sliced lemon and melted butter. Be sure to send them to table on the slices of toast on which they were cooked, for if the toast has been placed cunningly and well, it will have caught all the trail, which will have cooked to perfection. The roasting pan may be swilled out with a very little good stock, to form a gravy for those who require it.

FOOTNOTE: If you should happen to hit a crow instead of your snipe, bury the bloody thing.

TO TRUSS A SNIPE:

Skin the bird, head and all; use the beak and head to skewer through the legs and tie the feet together.

Desserts

PAVLOVA CAKE

CLIFFORD GRANT

4 egg whites
8 ounces sugar
½ teaspoon cream of tartar
½ teaspoon vanilla
1 teaspoon vinegar
½ pint whipping cream
    strawberries, pineapple or passion fruit

Whip whites of eggs until stiff. Gradually add sugar, beating well.
Add vanilla and cream of tartar. Add vinegar. Pile mixture onto
oven sheet that has been well greased. Cook in slow oven (gas
250°) ¾-1 hour. Allow to stand a few minutes. Turn on to serving
dish (bottom-side up). Cover with whipped cream when cool.
Garnish with strawberries, chopped pineapple, or passion fruit.

MOUSSE DE CHOCOLAT

BIDU SAYAO

1 6 oz. package of semisweet chocolate
    pieces
2 whole eggs
2 tablespoons of instant coffee
2 tablespoons of Grand Marnier Liqueur
¾ cup of milk

Put all ingredients into blender. Bring milk to a boil and add milk
to all ingredients. Cover blender, turn to high speed for 2 minutes
only. Pour into cups and top with whipped cream. Put in ice box
for 4 hours before serving.
    Serves six people.

DREAM BALLS

QUERITA EYBEL

½ cup butter
2 tablespoons sugar
1 teaspoon vanilla
1 cup cake flour
1 cup chopped pecans or walnuts
 a pinch of salt

Cream the butter; add sugar and the other ingredients. Roll into small balls. Bake for 15-20 minutes in a moderate oven (350°). Roll the cookies in powdered sugar while they are still hot.

Makes about twenty-seven cookies. They are superb.

FRULATO
(A FRUIT AND ICE CREAM DRINK)

KEN MALUCELLI

In a blender, combine your favorite canned and/or fresh fruits. The fruitier the better. Fresh bananas and strawberries with a can of apricots or plums, peaches, etc. Also: maraschino cherries, fresh lemon, grated or diced lemon peel.

Mix in blender a few seconds. Add several scoops of vanilla ice cream. You can, if you like, fill your entire blender with fruits and ice cream.

Serve in tall beer mugs with slice of orange, sprig of fresh mint or any fruit garnish you prefer.

OATMEAL CAKE

ORVA HOSKINSON

1 *cup Quaker Quik oatmeal*
½ *cup shortening*
1 *cup dark brown sugar*
1¹/₃ *cups flour*
½ *teaspoon salt*
1 *cup white sugar*
3 *beaten eggs*
1¼ *cups boiling water*
1 *teaspoon baking soda*
½ *teaspoon cinnamon*

Soak the oatmeal in the boiling water and let the mixture stand for twenty minutes. Cream ½ cup of shortening, 1 cup brown sugar, the cup of white sugar and add the three beaten eggs. Sift together the flour, baking soda, salt and cinnamon and add to the oatmeal and sugar mixture. Bake for 30 minutes in a 350° oven in a greased pan.

BROIL ON ICING FOR OATMEAL CAKE

ORVA HOSKINSON

1 *stick melted butter*
¼ *cup heavy cream*
1 *cup chopped coconut*
1 *cup dark brown sugar*
1 *cup walnuts or pecans*
1 *teaspoon vanilla*

Mix the above ingredients together and spread on the cake after the cake is done. Brown the icing under the broiler for a few minutes.

SOUR CREAM CUSTARD PIE

ARIEL BYBEE

1 *quart sour cream*
1 *quart heavy whipping cream*
½ *cup sugar*
8 *ounces dry (regular, not instant) vanilla pudding*
2 *pie shells*

Whip the cream. Fold in sour cream. Combine sugar and pudding. Mix all of the ingredients together and beat with an electric mixer until smooth and thick. Divide the filling into two eight to nine inch pie shells. chill at least four hours or overnight. Serve topped with fresh fruit or fruit topping.

ABSOLUTELY HEAVEN!

CHERRY CHEESECAKE PIE

DONNA PETERSEN

1 *prepared graham cracker crust, chilled*
1 *large package Philadelphia cream cheese*
1 *large can sweetened condensed milk*
¼ *cup lemon juice*
½ *can pie cherries*
1 *teaspoon vanilla*

Soften the cream cheese, smoothing with a hand mixer, and add the sweetened condensed milk, lemon juice and vanilla. Pour mixture into the chilled crust and chill an additional 2 hours. Before serving, top the pie with the cherries.
   Serves eight.

BLITZEN TORTE

RICHARD MUNDT

BATTER:

    ½ cup butter
    4 egg yolks
    1 cup cake flour
    1 tablespoon vanilla
    ½ cup sugar
    4 tablespoons milk
    1 teaspoon baking powder

Combine all the ingredients and pour them into two greased cake tins. Bake 20 minutes at 350°.

FILLING:

    2 cups milk
    1 egg, slightly beaten
    1 teaspoon vanilla
      chopped walnuts
    2 tablespoons sugar
    1 tablespoon cornstarch
    4 egg whites, beaten until stiff with 1 table-
      spoon sugar.

Make a custard of the milk, sugar, egg, cornstarch and vanilla. Cook over low heat, stirring constantly until thickened. Spread this mixture over the bottom layer of the cake. Spread the top layer with the beaten egg whites, with 1 tablespoon sugar, then sprinkle with the chopped walnuts. Bake just this top layer in a 350° oven until the meringue has browned. Combine the two layers, and there you have it.

BACHELOR'S CAKE

KEN MALUCELLI

2 *cups all purpose flour*
2 *cups sugar*
2 *teaspoons baking powder*
½ *teaspoon salt*
1 *cup broken walnuts*
2 *eggs*
1 *#303 can fruit cocktail and its juice (or 1 can #303 of your favorite fruit: pineapple wedges, quartered apricots, plums, peaches, etc.)*

TOPPING:

1 *cup evaporated milk*
1 *cube butter or margerine*
  maraschino cherry bits
1½ *cups sugar*
1 *teaspoon vanilla*

Heat oven to 350°. Use cake pan which comes with its own cover, as cake must cure for at least 24 hours. Grease and flour oblong cake pan, 13"x9½"x2". In a large bowl combine all dry ingredients and stir. Blend in eggs and can of fruit and juice. NO BEATING NECESSARY!! Pour into pan and bake 50 minutes or until wooden pick inserted in center of cake comes out clean. Remove from oven, prick top of cake all over and pour on hot topping. Sprinkle on bits of maraschino cherry and dribble on a little maraschino juice if desired. Cool and cover pan. Store.

TOPPING: Combine milk, margarine and sugar in saucepan. Bring to boil. Boil 2 minutes. Remove from heat. Add vanilla. Pour over hot cake.

MORNING FRUIT BREAD

KEN MALUCELLI

1 *can purple plums*
1 *can apricot halves*
1 *can sliced peaches*
1 *cup chopped nuts*
1 *cup raisins*
1 *small bottle maraschino cherries*
1 *package (13 oz.) hot roll mix prepared according to package directions. Let rise until doubled.*
½ *cup melted butter*
¾ *cup sugar with 1 teaspoon each of cinnamon, nutmeg, allspice*

Pour all fruit into collander with large bowl underneath to collect and keep juices. Cut fruit into smaller peices, or "half-halves". Discard pits.

After dough rises, about 30 minutes, roll out on floured board to about 15"x18". Brush with melted butter. Sprinkle with sugarspice mixture.

Cut dough into 3" squares. Into each square place a few pieces of fruit and nuts. Fold and seal edges of each fruit pocket and layer in a greased 9"x5" loaf pan. Between each layer sprinkle on a few nuts and maraschino cherry bits. Let rise 30 minutes or so. Bake in 350° oven 35-45 minutes or until dark golden. Brush with fruit glaze.

FRUIT GLAZE: *Combine about 2 cups reserved syrup with 2 tablespoons sugar. Let cool a little before brushing over bread.*

Left over fruits and juices can be combined to make a delicious Frulato.

GRANITA DI CAFFE
(Coffee Ice)

EVELYN LEAR & THOMAS STEWART

1 *scant cup sugar (or, preferably, castor sugar)*
2 *cups water*
2 *cups extra-strong coffee or espresso*
1 *cup heavy cream, whipped*

Dissolve the sugar in the water and combine with the coffee. Pour into freezing tray and freeze until the mixture reaches a mushy stage. Stir several times during this process. The granita must not freeze too hard and won't, if you have used enough sugar. Place a heaping tablespoon of whipped cream on the bottom of each sherbet glass and then a few tablespoons of the sherbet. Alternate the cream and sherbet, topping with whipped cream. Serve at once.

Serves four to six.

Anyone who has been to Italy is probably familiar with this coffee ice, usually served with whipped cream. This dessert has the virtue of being truly Italian, and yet it can be made anywhere. The trick is to stir the mixture occasionally during the freezing process. If you want your granita to taste exactly like the Italian product, alternate layers of the coffee ice with whipped cream. It is a cool, cool dessert and quite different from most sherbets. A granita is also served without whipped cream in Italy. For a unique touch, you might add just a few drops of a coffee liqueur.

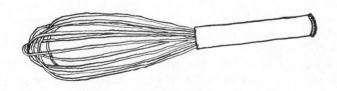

BLACK BOTTOM PIE

JOHN ALEXANDER

CRUST:

   14 *gingersnaps*
   5 *tablespoons melted butter*

BOTTOM FILLING:

   2 *cups milk*
   4 *egg yolks, beaten well*
   ½ *cup sugar*
   1½ *tablespoons cornstarch*
   1½ *ounces unsweetened chocolate*
   1 *teaspoon of vanilla extract*

TOP FILLING:

   1 *tablespoon gelatin*
   2 *tablespoons hot water*
   4 *egg whites*
   ½ *cups sugar*
   ½ *teaspoon cream of tartar*
   2 *tablespoons whiskey or brandy*

To make CRUST, roll out gingersnaps with a rolling pin to make fine crumbs. Stir in melted butter. Pat crumb mixture into a 9-inch pie pan. Bake in a 400° oven 10 minutes. Cool thoroughly.

To make FILLING, scald 1¾ cups of milk. Stir the beaten egg yolks into the milk, then stir in the sugar. Dissolve the cornstarch in the remaining ¼ cup cold milk and stir into the hot mixture. In the top of a double boiler over simmering water, cook filling 20 minutes, stirring constantly, or until mixture coats the spoon. Remove from heat and measure out 1 cup. In a mixing bowl, combine the 1 cup custard with the chocolate, add the vanilla and beat well until mixture cools slightly and chocolate melts. Pour into pie shell and chill.

To make TOP FILLING, dissolve the gelatin in the hot water and add to remaining custard. Let cool. Meanwhile, in a mixing bowl beat egg whites until foamy. Add some of the sugar and the cream of tartar. Beat until stiff, gradually adding remaining sugar. Stir whiskey into cooled custard and fold in beaten egg whites. Mound mixture on top of chocolate filling and chill. Garnish with shavings of bitter chocolate.

ALMOND BAVAROIS WITH CHOCOLATE SAUCE

HENRY MC GUCKIN

2 *cups milk*
²/₃ *cup of sugar*
   pinch of salt
½ *cup finely ground almonds*
4 *teaspoons gelatin, soaked in ½ cup cold milk*
1 *teaspoon almond flavoring*
1 *cup whipping cream*

On top of double boiler, heat milk, sugar, salt. When hot, add almonds. Remove from heat. Cover and let stand for 15 minutes. Add gelatin soaked in cold milk and heat mixture, just until gelatin is dissolved. Cool. Add almond flavoring. Place in the refrigerator until mixture has thickened. Beat with rotary beater until fluffy. Beat whipping cream until stiff and fold it gently but thoroughly into the mixture. Spoon into a 5 cup ring mold, lightly greased. When firm, (it takes several hours and it is a good idea to prepare this the night before), unmold on a flat dish. Dribble some of the chocolate sauce over the ring and sprinkle ground or slivered almonds on top. Serve with more sauce if desired.

   Serves six to eight.

SAUCE:

²/₃ *cup milk*
1½ *square unsweetened chocolate cut up*
4 *tablespoons sugar*
   pinch of salt
1 *tablespoon cornstarch*
1 *teaspoon vanilla*

On top of double boiler heat milk, chocolate and pinch of salt. When chocolate is melted, blend well and add sugar. Stir until it is dissolved. Thicken sauce with the cornstarch which has been mixed with a little cold water, stirring constantly until mixture has thickened to desired consistency. Cool. Flavor with vanilla. Refrigerate.

VANILLEKIPFERL
(VANILLA CRESCENTS)
KURT HERBERT ADLER

    1 *cup, less 2 tablespoons butter*
2½ *cups all purpose flour*
  ½ *cup sugar*
  ½ *cup blanched almonds, ground*
    2 *egg yolks*
  ½ *teaspoon vanilla*
       powdered sugar

Have all ingredients as cold as possible. Cut all the butter into 2½ cups of flour sifted with ½ cup of sugar. Add ½ cup almonds, the egg yolks, and the vanilla and work the ingredients into a smooth dough. Chill dough for at least 1 hour. Roll into strips about the thickness of a finger and cut the strips into two inch pieces. Roll out each piece until it is three inches long and curve it into a crescent. Bake in a slow (300 ° F.) oven on a buttered baking sheet for about 20 minutes until cookies are dry and faintly colored. Sprinkle a plate heavily with powdered sugar. With a spatula transfer cookies to the plate and sprinkle with more powdered sugar. These go well with fruit or sherbet for dessert. A delicate after dinner cookie.

Makes about forty.

CZECH FRUIT DUMPLINGS

SONA CERVENA

DOUGH:

 8 *ounces creamed cottage cheese*
 2 *eggs - slightly beaten*
 2 *cups* Wondra *Flour (no substitutions)*
   salt

FILLING:

Fruit in season—plums, apricots, strawberries

TOPPING:

Sugar and melted butter OR
Sugar, cinnamon and melted butter

Mix the dough well and leave it in the refrigerator for at least one half hour. Sprinkle the board with a little bit of flour to avoid sticking and roll out the dough into a layer 1/6 inch thick. Cut into squares according to size of the fruit and wrap around the fruit, forming balls with your hands (use again a little bit of flour to avoid sticking). Put the dumplings—all at the same time in plenty of rapidly boiling water and boil for five to ten minutes—again according to size and hardness of fruit. Serve immediately, topped with sugar and melted butter.

 Serves three - meal.
 Serves six - dessert.

GREEK STYLE COOKIES

IRENE DALIS

4½ cups flour
1 pound sweet butter
¾ cup confectioners' sugar (use more for storage)
1½ tablespoons brandy
2 teaspoons vanilla
whole cloves (optional)

Sift flour twice. Cream butter until it has the consistency of satin. (Old recipes say beat one hour, but a fraction of this with the electric beater will do the trick). Sift sugar and gradually work in flour; use 4 cups at first, adding the remaining ½ cup if the dough seems too moist after chilling. Cover and refrigerate for one hour. Pinch off bits of dough and form into round cookies about the size of a thick half-dollar. Place on unbuttered baking sheet and bake in a slow 325° oven until sand-colored (not brown) for about 20 minutes. Cool on baking sheet. Place a clove in each cookie; sprinkle with more confectioners' sugar, and store in an airtight tin box.

Makes about 4 dozen cookies.

SOUTHERN PECAN PIE

GEORGE LONDON

CRUST:
   1 *cup flour*
   ⅓ *cup chortening*
   ½ *teaspoon salt*
   2 *tablespoons ice water (approx.)*

Add salt to flour; cut in shortening and blend until it is the consistency of coarse corn meal. Add ice water until the dough just holds together. Roll out on floured surface, fit into a 9-inch pie pan and crimp edges.

FILLING:
   ½ *cup white sugar*
   ½ *teaspoon salt*
   2 *tablespoons flour*
   3 *tablsepoons soft butter*
   2 *large eggs*
   1 *cup light corn syrup*
   1 *cup pecan halves*
   1 *teaspoon vanilla*

Mix flour and sugar together, add salt, blend in butter and lightly beaten eggs until well mixed. Add corn syrup, pecans and vanilla and stir until completely blended. Pour into prepared pie shell. Place in 400° oven for 10 minutes, then lower oven temperature to 350° and continue to bake for approximately 40 minutes, until center of filling is set.

ROMANIAN WALNUT CROISSANT

STELLA ROMAN

This is my favorite dessert and coffee cake.

Mix in a bowl one pound of sweet butter and one cup of sugar, ½ teaspoon of salt, and mix well. Add 4 egg yolks, one cake of yeast (which was soaked in ¼ cup of warm milk). Also add about ½ pint of sour cream and work all these ingredients together . Allow the dough to rest for one hour in a warm place.

In the meantime, in a cooking pan prepare the filling by putting one pound of ground walnuts mixed with very little milk and one cup of sugar or more. Add a little lemon juice and lemon rind and a cup of raisins.

When I want to be fancy, I add a little liqueur of Triple Sec (orange) or Grand Marnier or Remy Martin to the filling mix and warm for a few minutes on the stove and then cool.

Place dough on the board, cut pieces the size of an egg and roll out each separately; put one teaspoon of filling in one corner of each piece. Roll up the dough and shape it like a horseshoe with your fingers. Place cookies on a greased baking sheet and paint each one with egg yolk and a little milk mixture (use a cooking brush). Let rest for an hour and paint again. Bake for 35 to 45 minutes at 350° until light brown.

DELICIOUS!!   BON APETIT!!

Menu

Curtain Call

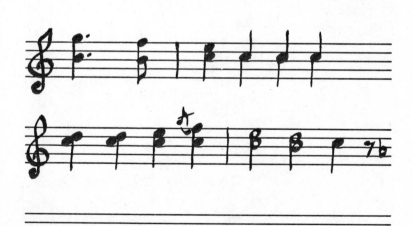

ORIGINAL JOE'S CLAM CHOWDER

ENJOYED BY ARCHIE DRAKE

4 *1 pound cans chopped clams*
1 *quart clam juice*
6 *large potatoes, cubed*
6 *large chopped onions*
3 *stalks celery, cubed*
4 *leeks, sliced fine*
2 *cups olive oil*
2 *16-ounce cans of tomato puree or sauce*
1 *teaspoon salt*
2 *large garlic cloves, chopped*
½ *teaspoon tarragon*
1 *teaspoon thyme*
  tabasco

Saute garlic in olive oil in a 6 quart pot. Add onions, celery, leeks, tarragon and thyme. When browned, add tomato puree, clams, and the clam juice. Bring to a boil and add salt, a few drops of tabasco, and the cubed potatoes. Simmer until the potatoes are done.

Serves four.

ORIGINAL JOE'S OSSO BUCCO

ENJOYED BY ARCHIE DRAKE

6 *large, or 12 small veal shanks, cut 1½ inches thick*
2 *16-ounce cans tomatoes*
6 *large onions, chopped*
2 *garlic cloves, chopped*
2 *stalks celery, cubed*
2 *pounds mushrooms, sliced*
½-1 *cup olive oil*
1 *teaspoon Italian seasoning*
1 *teaspoon rosemary*
beef stock to cover
garlic salt, salt and pepper to taste
cornstarch
white wine

Place veal shanks flat in an oven pan. Sprinkle with garlic salt, salt, pepper, rosemary, and a little olive oil. Braise in a moderate oven (350°) until brown on both sides.

While meat is in the oven, brown garlic in olive oil, using a 4-quart pot. Add onions, celery, mushrooms and seasoning. Cook until tender. Add tomatoes, salt, and pepper. Bring to a boil, and then let simmer. Drain the liquid from the braised veal shanks and place in a shallow pan. Pour the sauce over the meat, and add enough broth to cover. Let simmer until the meat is tender. Thicken liquid with cornstarch diluted in white wine, and let simmer a few more minutes. Serve with risotto (rice).

Serves six.

KUO WAH CRISP FRIED WON TON WITH SWEET AND SOUR SAUCE

FILLING:

½ *lb pork*
¼ *lb shrimp (shelled and deveined)*
6 *water chestnuts, fresh or canned*
2 *green onions*
1 *teaspoon sugar*
1 *tablespoon soy sauce*
½ *teaspoon salt*
1 *teaspoon sherry*
pinch of pepper

Grind, or chop fine, pork, shrimp, water chestnuts and green onions. Then mix well with sugar, soy sauce, salt, sherry and pepper.

Fresh won ton wrappers may be purchased by the pound from Chinese grocers or noodle factories. They are approximately three inches square. Any unused won ton skins may be tightly wrapped and frozen for later use.

HOW TO FILL WON TON:

Place the won ton skin flat on a board so that it has a diamond shape. Use the narrow end of a single chop stick to place ⅓ teaspoon filling in the corner farthest from you. Roll the won ton loosely toward you, leaving the chop stick inside. When you have rolled as far as the center (or widest part of the diamond), remove the chop stick. Use it to moisten the wide corners with a dab of water. Press these two wide corners together, stretching up and back in a direction directly opposite from the corner that was nearest you. Keep won ton refrigerated and covered with damp cloth.

TO FRY:

Deep fry in peanut or vegetable oil at 375° for two to three minutes, until golden. Keep hot in warm oven until ready to serve. Serve with hot sweet and sour sauce.

SWEET AND SOUR SAUCE:

1 *cup water*

²/₃ cup brown sugar

¹/₃ cup vinegar

4 or 5 drops red coloring

3 tablespoons catsup

¼ teaspoon salt

¼ teaspoon powdered Jamaican ginger (or 2 slices fresh ginger)

2½ tablespoons cornstarch, dissolved in ½ cup water, stirred and cooked until thickened and clear

Stir and heat to boiling all ingredients except cornstarch. Add dissolved, thickened, clear cornstarch after other ingredients have reached boiling point.

Optional addition to Sweet and Sour Sauce: pineapple tidbits, maraschino, and/or canned lichee may be added just before serving for added taste and eye appeal.

As enjoyed at Kuo Wah Restaurant in San Francisco by Raymond Manton.

CAFE BRULOT

BRUCE YARNELL
JOAN PATENAUDE

4 oz. cognac
8 whole cloves
2 tablespoons chocolate syrup
2 long strips lemon peel
2 small cinnamon sticks
10 pieces lump sugar
2 long strips orange peel
2 cups strong black coffee

Pour all ingredients, except hot coffee, into chafing dish. Ignite cognac with match and stir ingredients until well blended. After a minute or two slowly pour in hot black coffee and continue to stir. (In winter, heat the cognac before using.)

To serve, strain into demitasse cups.

HOLLANDAISE SAUCE

BEVERLY SILLS

3 egg yolks
¼ pound soft butter
2 tablespoons lemon juice
salt

Mix above ingredients in blender for 5 seconds. While in blender add 4 tablespoons of hot water. Place in top of double boiler. Beat with whisk over simmering water until thickened. Add paprika as garnish.
Serves four.

FAVOURITE RESTAURANT IN SAN FRAN-CISCO

MICHAEL LANGDON

House of Prime Rib, Van Ness Avenue.

Roast Beef, cooked through and sliced English fashion, with an Idaho baked potato and creamed spinach. It is excellent with a glass of good red wine.

SUMMER DISH AT HOME IN ENGLAND

MICHAEL LANGDON

> *Sussex crab*
> *salt and pepper*
> *malt vinegar*

Mince crab to a fine consistency and serve it on a very cool plate. Flavor it simply with salt, pepper and a few drops of malt vinegar. Serve with a side salad of:

> *crisp lettuce*
> *cucumber*
> *sliced tomatoes*

Accompany this light meal with a glass of chilled hock.

LEONTYNE PRICE

CONNIE WILLIAMS WEST INDIAN RESTAURANT

Black Velvet, Hors d'oeuvres

Sherry Black Bean Soup

African Chicken in Peanut Butter

   Steamed Rice
   African Kale

Connie's Special Coconut Bread

Tossed Green Salad

   West Indian Salad Dressing

Tropical Pudding with Rum Sauce

Almaden Burgundy Wine

MENU

ANJA SILJA

TRADER VIC'S
TONGA
SPARERIBS

SQUAB WITH WATER CHESTNUTS

KIWI OR LEMON SHERBET WITH GINGER

INDEX:

Almond Bavarois 112
Amish Cabbage with Sour Cream 45

Bachelor's Cake 107
Beef:
    Beefsteak Woronoff 68
    Bourguinon 80
    Pepper Steak 64
    Roast Beef, House of
        Prime Rib 125
    Smothered Steak Roll-ups 69
    Stuffed Cabbage 88
    Szedi Gulyas 73
Beef Tea 15
Beet and Endive Salad 43
Bermuda Drink 14
Blender Caesar Salad Dressing 44
Black Bottom Pie 110
Blitzen Torte 106
Bourex (Cheese Pastry Fingers) 16
Broil-on-Icing 104
Bulghour Pilaf 50

Cabbage, Amish with Sour Cream
    and Bacon 45
Cabbage, Stuffed 88
Cafe Brulot 124
Cake:
    Bachelor's 107
    Blitzen Torte 106
    Oatmeal 104
    Pavlova 102
Cannelloni 56
Carrot, Sweet Potato and
    Prune Tzimmes 33
Caponatina 18
Casalinga (chicken liver spread) 19
Caesar Salad 44
Cherry Cheesecake Pie 105

Chicken:
    and Lobster Cantonese   74
    and Pear Mousse   87
    Bombay   81
    in the Pot   72
    Pollo a lo Agridulce   79
    Poulet a Couchet Blanche   95
    Standing Room Chicken   83
    Surprise   75
Clam Chowder, Original Joe's   120
Crab:
    . . Cake Puffs   22
    . . Casserole   82
    Divine Casserole   84
    Fresh . . . Dish   90
    Favorite Summer Dish   125
    . . . Imperial Casserole   98
Creme de Tomate Marie-Louise   30
Cold Pea Soup   26
Cold Tomato Soup   26
Cookies (Greek Style)   115
Corn Chowder   28
Croissant, Romanian Walnut   117
Czech Fruit Dumplings   114

Dill and Mustard Sauce,
  for Salmon   76
Dill and Pepper Cured Salmon   76
Dolmades with Lemon Sauce   89
Dream Balls   103

Egg Noodles ala Bolognese   59
Eggplant:
    Caponatina   18
    . . . Pizzas   21
Endive and Beet Salad   43
Endive Salad, Hot   39
Epicurean Cocktail   14

Favorite Summer Dish   125
Filet of Sole   68

Florian Fruit Salad	42
Frulato	103
Granita di Caffe	109
Greek Salad	40
Hollandaise Sauce	124
Italian Delight	49
Keftethakia, Malas	20
Keftethakia, Dalis	23
Lasagna, Fish Sauce	58
Linguine:	
alla Licia Albanese	60
with White Clam Sauce	52
Linsensuppe (Lentil Soup)	32
Litvak	14
Matagliati con Fagioli	61
Meistersalad, Die	36
Mexican Salad	38
Morning Fruit Bread	108
Moussaka	92
Mousse de Chocolat	102
Oatmeal Cake	104
Osso Bucco-Original Joe's	121
Oxtail in Wine	70
Pasta alla Tito Gobbi	53
Pavarotti Cocktail	14
Pavlova Cake	102
Pecan Pie, Southern	116
Pepper Steak	64
Persian Rice with Almonds	48
Pollo a lo Agridulce	79
Pork Loin and Red Cabbage	64
Potato Kugel	41
Poulet a Couchet Blanche	95

Ravioli, Lamb filled	78
Risotto Milanese	55
Roast Snipe	99
Rock Cornish Hens	96
Romanian Walnut Croissant	117
Russian or Oriental Eggplant	42
Salmon, Dill and Pepper Cured	76
Saltimbocca ala Mosli	71
Shrimp:	
a la Sze	17
Creole in Spinach and	
Rice Ring	94
Tempura	93
Smothered Steak Roll-ups	69
Snipe, Roast	99
Snitz and Knepp	65
Sole, Filet of	68
Soup:	
Clam Chowder, Original	
Joe's	120
Cold Pea	26
Cold Tomato	26
Corn Chowder,	
Pennsylvania-Dutch	28
Creme de Tomate	
Marie-Louise	30
Linsensuppe (Lentil Soup)	32
Sour Cream Potato	28
Tutmaj (Yogurt Soup)	31
Yogurt Soup	27
Sour Cream Custard Pie	105
Sour Cream Potato Soup	28
Spaghetti:	
alla Capobianco	50
alla Matriciana	54
Standing Room Chicken	83
String Beans, Yugoslavian	37
Stuffed Cabbage	88
Sukiyaki on the Road	86
Szegedi Gulyas	73

Tempura	93
Tonno-Mariner's Style	85
Tuna:	
Tonno, Mariner's Style	85
Tutmaj (Yogurt Soup)	31
Tzimmes, Carrot, Sweet Potato	
and Prune	33
Vanilleknipferl	113
Veal Cutlets in Port	67
Welsh Cheese Pudding	67
Wonton with Sweet and Sour	
Sauce, Kuo Wah	122
Yogurt Soup	27